HOLDING FAST

HOLDING FAST

Dealing with Doubt in the Latter Days

Robert L. Millet

DESERET
BOOK

Salt Lake City, Utah

Library of Congress Cataloging-in-Publication Data

Millet, Robert L.
    Holding fast : dealing with doubt in the latter days / Robert L. Millet.
        p.   cm.
    Includes bibliographical references (p.   ) and index.
    ISBN 978-1-59038-919-5 (paperbound)
    1. Spiritual life—The Church of Jesus Christ of Latter-day Saints.
2. Faith.   3. The Church of Jesus Christ of Latter-day Saints—Doctrines.
I. Title.
    BX8656.M543 2008
    248.4'89332—dc22   2008019641

Printed in the United States of America
Publishers Printing, Salt Lake City, UT

10   9   8   7   6   5   4   3   2   1

To Paul H. Peterson (1941–2007)

*valued friend, outstanding teacher, and personal mentor,
a man who faced questions with faithful optimism
and sought to instill faith all his days*

Into my heart, purified of all sin,
there entered a light which came from on high
and then suddenly, and in a marvelous manner,
I saw certainty succeed doubt.

CYPRIAN (A.D. 205–258)

CONTENTS

PREFACE

Some six months before his death and resurrection, Jesus and his three chief apostles—Peter, James, and John—descended the Mount of Transfiguration, no doubt contemplating the majesty and import of what they had just experienced. When they reached the bottom of the mount, they were immediately surrounded by a group of people who were a bit perplexed. A man had brought to the other members of the Twelve his son, who had a "dumb spirit," that is, a devil (Mark 9:17). The father had pleaded with the other apostles to cast out the evil spirit, but they had been unable to do so.

Jesus spoke tenderly to the grieving father, "If thou canst believe, all things are possible to him that believeth." Then came those wonderfully painful but honest and revealing words, a phrase that touches each one of us who falls short, who misses the mark, who wonders whether we have what it takes to be a full-fledged disciple of the Nazarene: "And straightway the father of the child cried out, and said with tears, *Lord, I believe; help thou mine unbelief*" (Mark 9:24; emphasis added).

The father's words are plain enough for a child to understand. They represent a genuine, heartfelt acknowledgment of personal weakness but a weakness no different and no more serious than many of us would feel on such an occasion.

Another rendering of this passage is as follows: "I do believe; *help me overcome my unbelief*" (New International Version, Mark 9:24; emphasis added). It is as though the father of the possessed child had uttered the following: "O Lord Jesus, you know all things. You know my heart. You know where I stand, and you know where I fall. You, above all others on this earth, know where and when I wander, how and in what manner I stray, and why I am lacking in faith. But I know who you are: you are the Christ, the Messiah, the Anointed One, the Son of the Living God, our Savior and Redeemer. You can do all things. You can heal the sick, cause the lame to walk, still the winds and the waves, and even raise the dead. I know that you can strengthen me, strengthen my faith; I know you can banish from my soul doubt and fear, that you can bestow faith that will make me whole."

This expression sets forth what we know well from other scriptures—that when we confess our weakness to him who has all power, we open ourselves to the Master's strength (see 2 Corinthians 12:8–10; Ether 12:27). It also highlights a vital verity: that each one of us finds ourselves somewhere along the continuum of faith— striving to know more surely, seeking to acquire a conviction that defies doubt, and longing to enter that settled conviction of the truth that disperses darkness and issues us into the rest of God.[1]

This book has been written to those who know and who know they know. It has been written to those who wonder, who have unanswered questions and unresolved issues. And it has been written to those who are solid in the faith but who want to gain that testimony, that quiet but comforting assurance, that serves as an anchor to the soul and a refuge of safety for those times—and, yes, they do come and will yet come— when the winds and storms of adversity beat with a fury upon our houses of faith. It is written for those who yearn to have a faith that is unshaken and unshakeable (see Jacob 7:5; Enos 1:11). We may not have all the answers, but we can be secure in our personal witness; we may not have a ready reply for every challenge, but we need not be troubled or discouraged or dislodged from the rock of our Redeemer.

In the preparation of this work, I am indebted to many students and faculty colleagues whose questions and suggestions have touched my heart, stretched my mind, and challenged me to achieve a simplicity beyond complexity, to articulate clearly why I know what I know. I am grateful for my treasured association with men and women who have come to know, by the power of the Holy Ghost, that Jesus Christ is the Son of the living God and that he was crucified for the sins of the world. I am grateful as well to those noble souls who have, for the time being, believed on their words and testimony. Both groups have charted a course leading to eternal life (D&C 46:13–14). In short, I am grateful for those who have chosen to believe.

I appreciate Cory H. Maxwell and the publication staff at Deseret Book Company for their encouragement and expertise. I especially thank my friend of many years, Suzanne Brady, whose simple but substantive editorial touch transforms a pretty good manuscript into a book an author is pleased to call his or her own.

Although I am indebted to many, many people through the years who have taught, counseled, chastened, and inspired me so that I could be in a position to write a book such as this, I take full responsibility for its content. I have sought diligently to write in a manner that would be in harmony with the teachings of holy scripture and the words of living prophets and apostles, but I alone am responsible for the conclusions drawn from the evidence cited. This work is not an official publication of either The Church of Jesus Christ of Latter-day Saints or Brigham Young University.

1

~~

THROUGH A GLASS DARKLY

In my younger days I heard members of the Church bear testimonies of every sort. One person would say, "I know that God answers prayers, for he has answered mine." Another would declare, "I know that revelation is real, for I have received revelation." A third might affirm, "I know that the atonement of Jesus Christ works, for I have had my own sins remitted. I know what it feels like to be pure."

As I reflect on those times, I realize that these were more than statements of belief or witnesses of a given doctrine. They were expressions of actual spiritual experiences Church members had enjoyed. Theirs wasn't simply an intellectual disclosure but rather a report of personal engagement with things divine.

A testimony of the gospel is a precious and priceless commodity; indeed, it is a necessary weapon in one's spiritual arsenal against the adversary. Because a veil of forgetfulness has been drawn across our minds and we cannot remember who we were and what we did before we were born, because we walk by faith and not by sight (2 Corinthians 5:7), because we cannot always see the end from the beginning, and because we now perceive reality through a glass darkly (1 Corinthians 13:12), we must, in this life, rely upon our spiritual sensitivity to things just beyond the veil and thus just out of reach of our conscious awareness.

Many things we once knew we are now relearning. "Our knowledge of persons and things before we came here," President Joseph F. Smith pointed out, "combined with the divinity awakened within our souls through obedience to the gospel, powerfully affects, in my opinion, all our likes and dislikes, and guides our preferences in the course of this life, provided we give careful heed to the admonitions of the Spirit.

"All those salient truths which come home so forcibly to the head and heart seem but the awakening of the memories of the spirit. Can we know anything here that we did not know before we came? Are not the means of knowledge in the first estate equal to those of this?"[1]

This is why a conversion to the faith is as much a reawakening as a discovery of new knowledge. Truly, one is converted "when he sees with his eyes what he ought to see; when he hears with his ears what he ought to hear; and when he understands with his heart what he ought to understand. And what he ought to see, hear, and understand is truth—eternal truth—and then practice it. That is conversion. . . . When we understand more than we know with our minds, when we understand with our hearts, then we know that the Spirit of the Lord is working upon us."[2]

Exercising faith in the Lord Jesus Christ, including faith in the divine purposes of the Father, "is not to have a perfect knowledge of things; therefore if ye have faith ye hope for things which are not seen, which are true" (Alma 32:21). Because we walk by faith, we learn to proceed in the face of the unknown, trusting resolutely that God is in his heavens and will orchestrate the events of our lives in such a way as to accomplish his purposes through us. We do so because we "know that all things work together for good to them that love God" (Romans 8:28). In a modern revelation we are beckoned to "search diligently, pray always, and be believing, and all things shall work together for your good, if ye walk uprightly and remember the covenant wherewith ye have covenanted one with another" (D&C 90:24).

As God's light shines in our internal individual souls, it shines also on things of eternal worth in the external world. That is to say, the light within points the way to go, the path to pursue, the avenue to trod. Contrary to a world immersed in pure naturalism, when we are alive with faith, then *believing is seeing.* C. S. Lewis, the great Christian writer who had such unusual insight into sacred matters, observed:

"I am certain that in passing from the scientific points of view to the theological, I have passed from dream to waking. Christian theology can fit in science, art, morality, and the sub-Christian religions. The scientific point of view cannot fit in any of these things, not even science itself. *I believe in Christianity as I believe that the Sun has risen, not only because I see it, but because by it I see everything else.*"[3]

A testimony is a precious gift of the Spirit, a sign that we have in fact been born again (1 John 5:1). It is a transition from darkness to light, from an aimless and wandering maneuver to a determined, Spirit-guided pursuit. We have put off skepticism and put on a believing heart. We have died as pertaining to cynicism and come alive as pertaining to gospel gladness and optimism.

We have put to death the old man of doubt and quick-ened the new man of assurance and certitude.

Those who keep an eye single to the glory of God (D&C 88:67) will eventually see with their eyes those things that they had formerly beheld only through the eyes of faith (Ether 12:19). The promise is sure to all who ask, seek, and knock: "If thou shalt ask, thou shalt receive revelation upon revelation, knowledge upon knowledge, that thou mayest know the mysteries and peaceable things—that which bringeth joy, that which bringeth life eternal" (D&C 42:61).

We must trust the Almighty to be true to his promises—to bring enlightenment when we have ques-tions, to provide perspective when we feel confused. No one needs to remain unsettled, unsatisfied, or unful-filled. And certainly no one needs to languish in doubt. God has provided a more excellent way.

2

INEVITABLE QUESTIONS

I have worked with the Church Educational System since 1975, beginning with seminaries and institutes and then joining the Brigham Young University religious education faculty in 1983. In other words, it has been my privilege and rich blessing to teach the gospel of Jesus Christ to thousands upon thousands of students, to see the light of truth enliven individuals and classes, and to become a living witness of the power of the word to transform human souls.

It would not be inappropriate to observe that the Church has made tremendous strides in the past thirty years in educating and preparing the Saints to know their religion, to understand the precepts and doctrines of salvation, including how to discover answers and find comfort within the pages of holy writ. I have always loved and respected my students, but I would not be honest if I did not point out that the students within my classrooms today are much more scripturally literate than when I began my work as a religious educator. This is a tribute to mothers and fathers who have made scripture study and gospel discussions high priorities in their homes, as well as to devoted teachers, advisers, and priesthood leaders who have set the example of drawing upon messages of enlightenment from the scriptures.

One does not, at least in good conscience, stroll into a university classroom and "wing it," as we sometimes say, particularly with eager and maturing minds who anticipate that the teacher will come prepared to deliver a message both spiritually strengthening and intellectually enlarging. In other words, as time has passed, I simply have had to work harder! My preparation has become more rigorous, my personal scripture reading has been more intense and reflective, and my own anticipation of what issues might be raised by bright, young Latter-day Saints has motivated me to pay a more significant price in preparation now than ever before.

In addition, over the past twelve years, I have been engaged in a work that has been both challenging and deeply rewarding. I have spent a significant percentage of my time in outreach, or interfaith relations, all in an effort to build friendships and bridges of greater understanding between Latter-day Saints and men and women of other faiths. I have read literally hundreds of books, watched a surprising number of DVDs, and listened to scores of CDs on such topics as Christian history and Christian theology, and in the process I have been comparing and contrasting, sifting and sorting. My mind has been stretched, my soul stirred, and my compassion deepened as I have had my eyes opened to the goodness and devotion of God-fearing people all over the world. I have gained a deeper appreciation for what they believe and why they behave as they do. In the process my faith in the restored gospel has deepened.

I say all of this to indicate that one cannot live in such an environment—reading and searching and digesting doctrinal and historical material over more than three decades—without some questions arising, questions of seeming inconsistencies, questions involving missing puzzle pieces, questions that may cause a bit of dis-ease, or discomfort, within me. Questions arise. Why? Perhaps it is the case that—

• I am thinking.

- My intellect is expanding.
- I am striving to love God with all my mind.
- Not everything has been revealed.
- I have not encountered everything yet.
- I have not paid a sufficient price to resolve the issue.
- I could be looking in the wrong places.
- There are other things I need to learn first.
- I am human and thus limited in my perspective.
- I am not God, who knows all things.

That's a good start at least. Asking questions is a natural part of being human. Children ask questions to better understand their world and to learn their limits. Teenagers ask questions because they want life to make sense and to be fair. College students ask questions because they are being exposed to many new ideas, some true and some false. Parents ask questions because they do not always know how to handle little traumas with young children or vexations of the soul with rebellious adolescents. Aged men and women ask questions because they want to know that their lives have counted for something and that their being on earth has made a difference somewhere, sometime. Questions, questions, and more questions are all around us.

Questions are not, in other words, unusual, inappropriate, or a sign of cynicism or even weakness. Consider some of the following questions, each of which is worthy of discussion:

- "Whom shall I send?" (God to all his spirit children) (Abraham 3:27)
- "Adam, where goest thou?" (God to our earthly father) (Moses 4:15)
- "Am I my brother's keeper?" (Cain to God) (Genesis 4:9)
- "How is it that thou canst weep?" (Enoch to God) (Moses 7:29)
- "Is anything too hard for the Lord?" (God to Abraham) (Genesis 18:14)
- "How long halt ye between two opinions?" (Elijah to ancient Israel) (1 Kings 18:21)
- "Knowest thou the condescension of God?" (an angel to Nephi) (1 Nephi 11:16)
- "Have ye inquired of the Lord?" (Nephi to his wayward brothers) (1 Nephi 15:8)
- "Whom say ye that I am?" (Jesus to the Twelve at Caesarea Philippi) (Matthew 16:15)

11

- "What good thing shall I do that I may have eternal life?" (a lawyer to Jesus) (Matthew 19:16)
- "My God, my God, why hast thou forsaken me?" (Jesus to the Father) (Matthew 18:46)
- "Why persecutest thou me?" (the risen Lord to Saul of Tarsus) (Acts 9:4)
- "Unto what were ye ordained?" (the Lord to his latter-day servants) (D&C 50:13)
- "O God, where art thou?" (Joseph Smith to God in the Liberty Jail) (D&C 121:1)

Asking questions can and should be a useful and productive enterprise whereby we gain knowledge, understanding, perspective, confidence, assurance, and boldness. There are obviously not a set number of questions to be addressed, after which we are fully equipped to face life once and for all. Rather, we change from moment to moment, from day to day, from year to year, and in the process we come to see life differently. A single answer may, and often does, result in a whole host of new questions. Because we walk by faith (2 Corinthians 5:7), because we see through a glass darkly (1 Corinthians 13:12), because we are not yet prepared to comprehend all of the solutions to life's issues and challenges, we ought not be startled or frightened when questions arise. Questions, when faced earnestly and with the proper spirit, are spiritually healthy.

Wouldn't it be wonderful if our questions, especially our questions about eternal things, would all be answered quickly, even instantaneously? Wouldn't it be delightful if answers to such matters as whom we should marry, what job offer we should accept, what counselors we should choose, what we should do to deal most effectively with a wandering child, what we should do to build a deeper sense of friendship and trust in our marriage, what would be the most important use of our time—and thousands of others—were clear and unambiguous or if God's response to our individual queries came within moments after our prayers? In some cases such answers do come. I have experienced that, and no doubt you have, too.

More often than not, however, the Almighty expects us to search and ponder and pray, to sift and sort and select, to wonder and wish and wait. Elder Richard G. Scott taught that answers to prayer seldom come while we are on our knees.[1]

A vital part of yielding our hearts unto God (Helaman 3:35) is surrendering to his timetable. He knows us best. He knows when and how and under what circumstances an answer should be given, when we are prepared to receive it, and at what point the divine response and counsel will be most cherished and then followed. To have faith in Christ is to trust him. To have faith in Christ is to have confidence in him. To have faith in Christ is to rely completely, wholly upon him (2 Nephi 31:19; Moroni 6:4). The Saints of the Most High are counseled to receive the word of truth "in all patience and faith" (D&C 21:5).

Those who have been involved in missionary work have witnessed again and again the miracle of testimony—those sacred revelations from heaven that come to men and women who have heard the message of salvation—and been stimulated by its ideas, stirred by its import, and confirmed in the faith through an answer to sincere prayer. In short, we have observed a human-divine interaction in which Spirit has spoken to spirit and in which an answer has come to the question, "Is it true?" On thousands of occasions people have knelt in prayer, poured out their hearts in supplication, been endowed with a light from on high, gained the witness of the Spirit, and arisen from their knees with an assurance and a resolve. The answer to their question came.

Once in a while the testimony one longs for is not so quick in coming. I want to share a story that I have told before but that seems to fit so beautifully here that it bears repeating. About thirty years ago I became acquainted with a lovely family that joined the Church—a mother, a father, and their young children. They seemed like perfect converts. They loved the Lord Jesus Christ, were drawn to the teachings of the Savior as found in The Church of Jesus Christ of Latter-day Saints, and were eager to jump in with both feet, eager to share their newfound way of life with others. I'll call them the Browns.

Sister Brown was quickly absorbed into the Primary while Brother Brown became fast friends with members of the elders quorum. After they had been in the Church well over a year, Brother Brown came to see me at my office one day. He expressed love for the Church as well as the thrill he felt at seeing his family deeply rooted in the gospel. Then he shared with me something that I never would have supposed. He did not really have a witness of Joseph Smith's prophetic calling.

In essence he said, "Bob, I love the restored gospel with all my heart. I know that if there is a true church, this is it. This is what I want for my family, now and forever. But I have a problem, one that won't go away: I just don't *know* that Joseph Smith was a prophet."

My friend then commented on how silly it must have sounded to me for him to embrace the revelation and at the same time be uncertain about the revelator.

He said, "I've prayed and prayed for a testimony of Joseph Smith, but I still can't say that I know he was called of God. I sincerely believe that he was a great and good man and that in the purest sense he was inspired of God. But I just don't know for sure that he was a prophet. What do I do?"

This was a bit unusual to me. From all I could discern, he harbored no rebellion, no duplicity, and no cynicism—only a simple and pure uncertainty. He wanted so badly to know, but he didn't know. He had questions.

We worked together on this problem for years. We read books on Joseph Smith, we fasted together, and we prayed together. In all that time, Brother Brown remained true and faithful. He labored in the auxiliaries of the Church and for a time served as elders quorum president. He and his family were active and involved in every way that could be expected of them. Our families grew quite close, and we often spent time talking about life and its challenges, about the central place of the gospel of Jesus Christ in our lives, and about where we would be if we were not members of the Church.

In time we moved from the area. Several years later I received a telephone call from Brother Brown. "Bob," he said excitedly, "I have something to tell you. I have a testimony of Joseph Smith. These feelings have been growing within me for some months now, but I can finally stand and say that I know, I *know!*"

I rejoiced with him as we talked about the peace of mind he had gained, and we discussed this phase of his lengthy but steady conversion. It had taken almost a decade for him to come to know, but in the interim he had done all that was expected of him. I have a witness of how much the Lord loves Brother Brown and all the other Brother and Sister Browns who have the spiritual stamina, moral courage, patience, and perspective to hold on to the rod, even when they are not absolutely certain about the destination of the path they traverse.

Once again there is no sin, no shame, and no stigma associated with having unresolved questions. Our Father in Heaven is not displeased with us when we wonder. Our Savior does not frown upon us when we wrestle with intellectual or spiritual dilemmas. And leaders of the Church do not consider us a defective disciple or less of a Latter-day Saint when we don't have all the answers. Life is all about learning. Mortality entails climbing the spiritual ladder toward celestial glory through growing in understanding "line upon line, precept upon precept, here a little and there a little" (2 Nephi 28:30; see Isaiah 28:10). One day we will "see as [we] are seen, and know as [we] are known" through having received of the Lord's fulness and of his grace (D&C 76:94).

For the time being, however, let us be grateful for what we *do* know, thankful that a gracious God has, in the words of the Prophet Joseph Smith, "created man with a mind capable of instruction, and a faculty which may be enlarged in proportion to the heed and diligence given to the light communicated from heaven to the intellect." Let us trust in the thrilling promise that "the nearer man approaches perfection, the clearer are his views, and the greater his enjoyments, till he has overcome the evils of his life and lost every desire for sin; and like the ancients, arrives at that point of faith where he is wrapped in the power and glory of his Maker and is caught up to dwell with Him."

We look forward to that unspeakable pleasure, resting patiently in an appreciation for the fact that "this is a station to which no man ever arrived in a moment: he must have been instructed in the government and laws of that kingdom by proper degrees, until his mind is capable in some measure of comprehending the propriety, justice, equality, and consistency of the same."[2]

And so we need to ask about whatever puzzles us, stretches us, or troubles us, for that is how we come to know. No invitation from our Lord is more frequently extended to his people than the entreaty to ask, seek, and knock (Matthew 7:7–8). Joseph Smith asked, and look what came of it!

Elder Bruce R. McConkie has written: "Young Joseph heard a sermon that dwelt upon these blessed words: 'If any of you lack wisdom, let him ask of God, that giveth to all men liberally, and upbraideth not; and it shall be given him.' (James 1:5.) A single sentence, twenty-six plain and simple words—these Spirit-authored words have had a great impact upon religion and all that appertains to it. Though they present a divine concept of universal application and were written for the guidance of all men, though they chart the course all must follow in their search for that religion which is pure and undefiled, and though they are a guide for all who seek the Lord and his saving truths— yet they were preserved through the ages for the especial guidance of that prophet who should usher in the dispensation of the fulness of times."[3]

We will not remain in ignorance forever, nor will that God who delights to honor those who serve him faithfully fail to endow the honest truth seeker with grander insight and deeper understanding (D&C 76:5–10). "How long can rolling waters remain impure?" the Prophet Joseph wrote in Liberty Jail. "What power shall stay the heavens? As well might man stretch forth his puny arm to stop the Missouri river in its decreed course, or to turn it up stream, as to hinder the Almighty from pouring down knowledge from heaven upon the heads of the Latter-day Saints" (D&C 121:33).

There is more to know, worlds more. There is comfort to be gained, sublime comfort. And there is eternal perspective to be acquired. God has all the answers. We just need to ask the right questions.

3

UNNECESSARY DOUBTS

During the time I served as director of one of the institutes of religion, a prominent family in the community joined the Church. The father was well known in the city as a successful businessman, and one of his sons was a popular athlete. The son began coming to institute and quickly became involved in the activities there—learning, serving, and having fun. After a year the family went to the temple, and all seemed well with them.

I asked the young man to serve as president of our institute, which he agreed to do. He was a natural leader, and he agreed to work closely with me in activating some of the single adults in the area who had slipped through the cracks into relative obscurity. We had a warm and congenial working relationship and often had long doctrinal chats as he sought to fill in many of the gaps in his gospel knowledge.

Several weeks passed, and we seemed to be making progress in our activation effort. Ray (not his real name) appeared to be finding great satisfaction in fellowship and discovery within his newfound faith. We generally met at 7 P.M. for a prayer meeting prior to our large Wednesday evening class. One Wednesday, Ray, rather uncharacteristically, arrived late. It didn't take a genius to observe that he was troubled, that something was clearly bothering him. We quickly made our plans for the evening, and I asked Ray to meet with me after class for a brief chat.

When we finally managed to get together about 10:30 P.M., I commented, "Ray, your mind seems to be elsewhere. Something's bugging you. What is it?"

"Oh, I'm just super tired," replied Ray, who was on the university football team. "The coach is working us pretty hard these days. I just need some rest."

Rest did not prove to solve his inner struggles, however, for his downcast, dejected, and distraught countenance continued week after week. Finally I managed to get Ray to open up.

"What's the deal?" I inquired. "You are obviously troubled about something. Don't you want to talk about it?"

He paused for a few moments, let out a long sigh, and said, "Brother Millet, our old minister came to visit my dad a few weeks ago. He began to attack Mormonism and left several pamphlets and videos with the family. Dad has now gotten caught up in this junk and has a ton of questions."

I suggested to Ray that perhaps his father might want to sit down and discuss the problem areas with me. Ray's face brightened for a moment, and he said, "Yea, maybe that would do it. I'll talk to him."

The next Wednesday night Ray came at 7:15 for prayer meeting but displayed much of the same despondency. He said, "Dad doesn't want to talk to any Latter-day Saints. He's working out things on his own."

Throughout the semester Ray tried to be upbeat and to throw himself into his institute assignment, but his heart just wasn't in it. He was going through the motions, but it was obvious that his worries about his father were consuming him. Then one institute night Ray stayed after class and made a startling announcement: "My dad wants the rest of the family to study the anti-Mormon stuff. In fact, he's insisting that we do so."

"Insisting?" I asked. "What does that mean?"

Ray looked up with teary eyes and answered, "Dad said if I refuse to read and listen to the materials the minister brought by, then I will need to leave home and find another place to live. What can I do? It looks like I have no other options."

"Yes, you do," I responded. "You can live with me and my family."

"Are you suggesting that it would be better to leave home?" he shot back.

"Well," I continued, "it's better than losing your faith."

"Losing my faith?" he echoed. "Is the material that bad? What's wrong? Is the Church hiding something?"

I assured him that the Church was not hiding anything but that anti-Mormonism, by its nature, is cutting and contentious, demeaning and demoralizing, repulsive to the Spirit of God, and poisonous to the heart.

"It will drag you down, fill you with unnecessary doubts, and dull your spirits. Don't study it. There's too much at stake here."

I wish that I could provide a happy ending for the story, but I cannot. Ray chose not to take my counsel. He read the vicious propaganda, found himself filled with doubts, let those doubts fester, refused to seek counsel or answers from the right sources, and consequently never returned to institute or to church. He allowed himself to be drawn into a web woven by angry people who perversely find delight in shaking the faith of others.

When, on scores of occasions, I have asked rabid anti-Mormons why they do what they do, it is not uncommon for them to reply with a sarcastic sneer: "Just trying to share the truth in love, sir." I believe the apostle Paul would roll over in his grave to know that individuals viciously and maliciously use his tender words (Ephesians 4:15) to accomplish malevolent motives.

The Savior counseled Joseph Smith and Oliver Cowdery, "Look unto me in every thought; doubt not, fear not" (D&C 6:36). Doubt not. What does that mean? What is it that the Master is warning against? What is it he would have us avoid? One approach to understanding doubt is to search the scriptures to see how the word is used throughout holy writ. Following are some examples.

1. Doubt is the antithesis, the opposite, of faith. "Jesus answered and said unto them, Verily I say unto you, *If ye have faith, and doubt not,* ye shall not only do this which is done to the fig tree, but also if ye shall say unto this mountain, Be thou removed, and be thou cast into the sea; it shall be done" (Matthew 21:21;

emphasis added). Note what the Prophet Joseph taught the School of the Elders: "Such is the weakness of man, and such his frailties, that he is liable to sin continually, and if God were not long-suffering, and full of compassion, gracious and merciful, and of a forgiving disposition, man would be cut off from before him, in consequence of which *he would be in continual doubt and could not exercise faith; for where doubt is, there faith has no power.*"[1]

The Prophet also taught that if men and women do not trust in the fact that our Heavenly Father is a God of justice, "they [will] be filled with fear and doubt lest the judge of all the earth would not do right, and thus *fear or doubt* [note here how they are equated], existing in the mind, *would preclude the possibility of the exercise of faith* in him for life and salvation."[2]

Finally, concerning the need for each person aspiring to complete Christian discipleship to be willing to sacrifice all things, Brother Joseph taught: "Those who have not made this sacrifice to God do not know that the course which they pursue is well pleasing in his sight; for whatever may be their belief or their opinion, it is a matter of doubt and uncertainty in their mind; and *where doubt and uncertainty are there faith is not, nor can it be. For doubt and faith do not exist in the same person at the same time;* so that persons whose minds are under doubts and fears cannot have unshaken confidence."[3]

Likewise, Moroni wrote concerning the brother of Jared: "And because of the knowledge of this man he could not be kept from beholding within the veil; and he saw the finger of Jesus, which, when he saw, he fell with fear; for he knew that it was the finger of the Lord; and he had faith no longer, for he knew, nothing doubting" (Ether 3:19).

2. Some of the meridian Apostles doubted the resurrection, even after the Savior had risen from the grave. "And when they saw him, they worshipped him: but some doubted" (Matthew 28:17). Here the word *doubt* seems to signify that they did not completely understand what they saw; they were perplexed, confused, startled, and probably mystified. This appears to be the same meaning of doubt in John 10:24: "Then came the Jews round about [Jesus], and said unto him, How long dost thou make us to doubt? If thou be the Christ, tell us plainly."

3. One form of *doubt* means to lose hope or to despair. "And now, when [Captain] Moroni saw that the city of Nephihah was lost he was exceedingly sorrowful, and began to doubt, because of the wickedness of the people" (Alma 59:11).

4. Sometimes *doubt* is used in scripture to signify ignorance or lack of understanding. For example, after the apostle Peter had received his vision of the unclean beasts three times—the vision signifying to him as head of the Church that the gospel of Jesus Christ should be taken to the Gentiles—he doubted. Luke writes, "Now while Peter doubted in himself what this vision which he had seen should mean, behold, the men which were sent from [the Roman centurion] Cornelius had made inquiry for Simon's house, and stood before the gate, and called, and asked whether Simon, which was surnamed Peter, were lodged there" (Acts 10:17–18). In other words, Peter was still uncertain what the vision meant; he wondered as to its central message.

5. Doubt can represent a person's negative reaction to something, a response leading to anger or contention. Paul wrote to Timothy, "I will therefore that men pray every where, lifting up holy hands, without wrath and doubting" (1 Timothy 2:8; compare D&C 60:7).

6. Doubt often signifies a spirit of resistance and hesitation, a wavering disposition. "If any of you lack wisdom, let him ask of God, that giveth to all men liberally, and upbraideth not; and it shall be given him. But let him ask in faith, nothing wavering [here wavering might just as well have been rendered as doubting

or hesitating]. For he that wavereth is like a wave of the sea driven with the wind and tossed. For let not that man think that he shall receive any thing of the Lord."

Now, attend to the important verse that follows: "A double minded man is unstable in all his ways" (James 1:5–8). This stirring and sobering counsel is similar to the Lord's counsel delivered through Joseph Smith: "He that doeth not anything until he is commanded, and receiveth a commandment with doubtful heart, and keepeth it with slothfulness, the same is damned" (D&C 58:29).

Why do people doubt? What are some common sources of doubt?

1. Some people doubt because they are not able to accept divine intervention, prophecy, or miracles. That is to say, they have limited their epistemology (their way of knowing) to the natural world—what can be experienced through the five senses or what can be observed, studied empirically, or replicated. Their map of the world is limited. To be straightforward, they are seeking directions from a deficient map. Their worldview has been sorely and severely circumscribed.

Sherem (Jacob 7) and Korihor (Alma 30) both denied prophecy and revelation, which means simply that they believed only what was within the natural world. Their counterparts, Jacob and Alma, accepted what was in the natural world but did not yield to the audacity or arrogance often associated with such attitudes as (1) "All I see is all there is" and (2) "You cannot know because I do not know." Their map was much larger, much more comprehensive in scope. They opened themselves to the supernatural world, a greater and grander world in which things are known and understood in very different ways.[4]

The fact is, our spiritual progress may be gauged largely by the extent to which we are willing to *see* some things through the eyes of faith. What we see for this time and season through the eyes of faith we will eventually see with anointed and glorified eyes (Alma 5:15; 32:41–43; Ether 12:19).

"Doubt is a perennial problem in the life of faith," Alister McGrath observed. "Doubt reflects our inability to be absolutely certain about what we believe. As Paul reminds us, we walk by faith, not by sight (2 Corinthians 5:7), which has the inevitable result that we cannot prove every aspect of our faith. This should not disturb us too much. After all, what is there in life that we can be absolutely certain about? We can be sure that 2 + 2 = 4, but that is hardly going to change our lives. The simple fact of life is that everything worth believing in goes beyond what we can be absolutely sure about."[5]

2. Some people doubt because they refuse to accept the demands of discipleship. In other words, their doubt disguises their spiritual laziness. They want an excuse not to get up early on Sunday mornings, not to go home teaching, not to pay tithing, not to spend three hours on Sunday in church meetings, not to work at the bishop's storehouse or the cannery, and so forth. They begin saying things such as, "I'm not sure I believe all this stuff anymore."

They solve their spiritual dissonance by convincing themselves, as well as others, that because they do not believe in the faith anymore, they need not abide by our Lord's exhortation to deny themselves, take up their cross daily, and follow him (Luke 9:23). In many cases I have been sorely tempted to ask those who claim that they no longer believe what they once believed, "And what commandment have you chosen not to keep?"

Some who acquire great learning come to feel a bit embarrassed about the plainness and simplicity of the Church. Some who have partaken of the fruit of the tree of life—have traversed the gospel path, held to the rod of iron, and partaken of the sweet fruits of the Atonement—give heed to the tauntings of the worldly wise and socially sophisticated.

"That person who thinks he has outgrown his church and his religion," President Harold B. Lee stated boldly, "has in reality proved himself too small to bear the responsibilities his membership entails and has shut himself up in his small intellectual world, and the vast treasures in the unseen world of spiritual truths are closed to his understanding."[6]

In that sense, doubt is a quiet form of gradual personal apostasy. "Is not apostasy a denial of that which was once genuinely known but which now comes to be doubted, discounted, and discarded? Neglected and unnourished, the tree of testimony is, alas, plucked up and cast out. But the tree was there, a fact to which its dried branches and roots are stark witness."[7]

3. Some people doubt because of issues of the faith, but the issues are matters about which they have paid little to know. We are called upon to be competent disciples, people who have a reason for the hope within them (1 Peter 3:15). Our religion should be as stimulating and satisfying to the mind as it is soothing and settling to the heart. Many members of the Church are eager to say that they "know the gospel is true" when they do not really know the gospel.

President Joseph F. Smith noted that one of the major sources of false doctrine is a group of people he calls the "hopelessly ignorant, whose lack of intelligence is due to their indolence and sloth, who make but feeble effort, if indeed any at all, to better themselves by reading and study; those who are afflicted with a dread disease that may develop into an incurable malady—laziness."[8]

On another occasion, President Smith condemned the bearing of one's testimony to "fill up the time in a public meeting" when there had been little preparation for a sermon or lesson. "Of those who speak in his name," President Smith declared, "the Lord requires humility, not ignorance."[9]

4. Some doubt because they are living in a state of unrepentant sin. Alister McGrath has written: "In part, doubt reflects the continued presence and power of sin within us, reminding us of our need for grace and preventing us from becoming complacent about our relationship with God. We are all sinners, and we all suffer from doubt, to a greater or lesser extent. . . . Sin causes us to challenge the promises of God, to mistrust him. . . . Our limitations as God's fallen and fallible creatures prevent us from seeing things as clearly as we would like." Sin prevents us from discerning "the big picture of the workings of God in the world."[10]

Isn't that an apt description of Laman and Lemuel's state? They "did murmur because they knew not the dealings of that God who had created them" (1 Nephi 2:12). On the other hand, Cyprian, bishop of Carthage and a great defender of the faith following the apostolic period, remarked, "Into my heart, purified of all sin, there entered a light which came from on high and then suddenly, and in a marvelous manner, I saw certainty succeed doubt."[11]

Once as a priesthood leader I sat opposite a member of the Church who had just moved into the ward. He asked to have his name removed from the records of the Church. When I asked him why, he responded, "Well, there are some serious doctrinal problems with Mormonism."

"Like what?" I asked.

"Oh," he said, "there are some pretty deep theological issues that I simply cannot reconcile, and I'm not sure you are in a position to know much about them."

He did not know me or what I did for a living, and so I said, "Why don't we try one or two issues to see if I can't help just a bit?" I pushed and pushed and pushed just to get him to volunteer one of the "deep theological issues," but he continued to put me off. Within an hour it was clear that the real problem was not intellectual but spiritual, for he had lived in wanton immorality for years. He didn't have questions about the doctrines of the Church but rather about his own ability to abide by gospel standards.

A final point to be made about doubt is that it is not really necessary. Elder John A. Widtsoe explained that there is a difference between "I have a question" and "I doubt." Each of us will have questions until we breathe our last breath. Mortality is a school, a proving ground where not all the answers to life's puzzle are in place or readily accessible. Questions arise. They just do. On the other hand, "Intelligent people cannot long endure . . . doubt," Elder Widtsoe stated. "It must be resolved. . . . We set about to remove doubt by gathering information and making tests concerning the subject in question. Doubt, then, becomes converted into inquiry or investigation.

"After proper inquiries, using all the powers at our command, the truth concerning the subject becomes known, or it remains unknown to be unravelled perhaps at some future time. The weight of evidence is on one side or the other. Doubt is removed. Doubt, therefore, can be and should be only a temporary condition. Certainly, a question cannot forever be suspended between heaven and earth; it is either answered or unanswered. As the results of an inquiry appear, doubt must flee. . . .

"The strong man is not afraid to say, 'I do not know'; the weak man simpers and answers, 'I doubt.' Doubt, unless transmuted into inquiry, has no value or worth in the world. Of itself it has never lifted a brick, driven a nail, or turned a furrow. To take pride in being a doubter, without earnestly seeking to remove the doubt, is to reveal shallowness of thought and purpose.

"Perhaps you are questioning the correctness of a gospel principle. Call it doubt if you prefer. Proceed to take it out of the region of doubt by examination and practice. Soon it will be understood, or left with the many things not yet within the reach of man. But remember: failure to understand one principle does not vitiate other principles."[12]

Helaman gave a glowing report of his two thousand stripling warriors when he wrote: "Now they never had fought, yet they did not fear death; and they did think more upon the liberty of their fathers than they did upon their lives; yea, they had been taught by their mothers, that *if they did not doubt, God would deliver them.* And they rehearsed unto me the words of their mothers, saying: *We do not doubt our mothers knew it"* (Alma 56:47–48; emphasis added).

God our Father does not expect perfect knowledge on the part of those who love and serve him; he who knows all things knows that we do not. What he does ask of us is not to surrender to our doubts. What he does call upon us to do is to pursue answers to questions, with trust in him and his anointed servants, and not to allow those questions to fester and morph into doubts. This exercise is not just about the intellect; it is also about the will. This challenge to deal faithfully with doubt is not about blind obedience; it is very much about trusting the Almighty and learning for this time and season to view all things with eyes of faith.

Elder Boyd K. Packer testified that "faith, to be faith, must center around something that is not known. Faith, to be faith, must go beyond that for which there is confirming evidence. Faith, to be faith, must go into the unknown. Faith, to be faith, must walk to the edge of the light, and then a few steps into the darkness. If everything has to be known, if everything has to be explained, if everything has to be certified, then there is no need for faith. Indeed, there is no room for it."[13]

As Joseph Smith taught, faith is a "principle of power."[14] One writer observed, "The Old Testament word for *faith* can be translated as 'being strong in the Lord.' Learn to trust in him, to commit the unknown future to the known care of the Lord."[15]

> *I will not doubt, I will not fear;*
> *God's love and strength are always near.*
> *His promised gift helps me to find*
> *An inner strength and peace of mind.*[16]

The risen Lord delivered a marvelous promise to his American Hebrews: "And *whosoever shall believe in my name, doubting nothing, unto him [or her] will I confirm all my words,* even unto the ends of the earth" (Mormon 9:25; emphasis added). The discipline and subsequent disposition to avoid doubt bring calm certitude, contagious conviction, and heavenly hope. There is supernal strength in believing. There is superhuman power that comes through trusting. There is sweet peace that flows from rejoicing in what we do know and looking ahead to what a merciful Heavenly Father will make known to us in his own time and in his own way (D&C 88:68).

4

SEASONS OF UNREST

I suppose I have heard the definition of the gift of the Holy Ghost as follows a hundred times: "The gift of the Holy Ghost is the right to the constant companionship of the third member of the Godhead, based upon our faithfulness." It's a good, solid explanation of the consummate privilege it is to have the Spirit as our guide and comforter throughout this life.

While eternal life, or exaltation, is the greatest of all the gifts of God to us in the eternal scheme of things (D&C 6:13; 14:7), the receipt of the Holy Ghost, given at the time of confirmation and administered by the laying on of hands, is a divine grace of immeasurable worth. "You may have the administration of angels," President Wilford Woodruff stated, "you may see many miracles; you may see many wonders in the earth; but I claim that the gift of the Holy Ghost is the greatest gift that can be bestowed upon man."[1]

The "constant companionship," the definition says. *Constant!* That word is a bit forbidding. Why? Because I know by personal experience that I do not enjoy a constant flow of revelation, a constant effusion of discernment, a constant sense of comfort and confidence, or a constant outpouring of peace and joy. Now, you may say, "That's easy to explain—you don't live in a manner that would entitle you to such manifestations of the Spirit." And you would be right.

On the other hand, although I have miles and miles to go before I rest, at least in terms of cultivating the gift and gifts of the Spirit as I should, I know something about the precious privilege it is to have the Spirit's direction and warmth. I know something about how vital it is to avoid ungodliness and worldly lusts. And I know too about how diligently I have tried to be a dedicated disciple of the only perfect being to walk this earth. In other words, while I am far from perfect, I have given my heart to God. I have turned my life to Christ. I have learned, through painful and sweet experience, to rely wholly upon my Redeemer for salvation. I guess you could say that I really do try to keep myself going in the commandment-keeping direction, knowing with a perfect certainty that the fulfillment I enjoy in this life and the eternal reward I receive in the life to come are a part of the mercy and grace promised to the followers of the lowly Nazarene.

Let's get to the point. My trust is in Jesus. My hope is in his atoning power to forgive my sins, cleanse my heart, transform my mind, and glorify my soul hereafter. I love him with all my mind and might and strength. Consequently, as an act of gratitude and as an expression of discipleship, I do my best to keep his commandments (John 14:15). But I do *not* always feel the Spirit the same way from moment to moment or from day to day.

There are times, I am sure, when you have had a magnificent and uplifting Sabbath, have partaken reverently and introspectively of the emblems of the sacrament, have been enlightened and motivated by the sermons and lessons, have searched the scriptures and discovered relevant new meaning, have knelt in prayer at the end of a supernal day and, with a fire burning in your heart, thanked God for his tender mercies—only to awaken the next day with a different feeling. As you awakened, you noticed that you did not feel the same Spirit you enjoyed only hours before. You were prompted to cry out, "What happened? Where did it go? What did I do? Was I wicked during the night without realizing it?"

Perhaps I am the only member of the Church to experience such a thing, but I don't think so. My guess is that each of us has had spiritual highs followed by spiritual lows, caused not by negligence, willful sin, negative attitudes, critical or murmuring dispositions, or anything we have done wrong. So what's going on?

I believe a part of the answer is contained in the conversation between Jesus and Nicodemus, as recorded in the New Testament. The Savior had just testified of the importance of the new birth, the spiritual birth that every man and woman must undergo to enter into the abundant life. "The wind bloweth where it listeth," Jesus said, "and thou hearest the sound thereof, but canst not tell whence it cometh, and whither it goeth: so is every one that is born of the Spirit" (John 3:8). It's a rather odd and unusual, even enigmatic passage, isn't it? Do we grasp what the Master is attempting to teach this brilliant and fastidious Pharisee who is somehow drawn to him?

The word translated here as *wind* is the Greek word *pneuma,* which may also (as in Hebrew) be rendered as *breath* or *spirit.* It is as if Jesus had said, "The Spirit goes where it will, and you can hear the sound [also rendered as *voice*], but you cannot always tell where it came from or where it is going. So it is with each person who has been born again." What's he trying to teach us?

For one thing, the Spirit of God is not under our immediate direction or control. It cannot be called here or sent there according to human whim. It cannot be manufactured, elicited, or produced whenever we as humans desire to do so. We can certainly set the stage. We can prepare properly, listen to uplifting music, search the scriptures, pray, and ask humbly for the Spirit's intervention or manifestation, but we cannot presume to determine the motions or movement of this sacred spiritual endowment.

"You cannot force spiritual things," Elder Boyd K. Packer said. "Such words as *compel, coerce, constrain, pressure, demand* do not describe our privileges with the Spirit. You can no more force the Spirit to respond than you can force a bean to sprout, or an egg to hatch before its time. You can create a climate to foster growth; you can nourish and protect; but you cannot force or compel: You must await the growth."[2]

Obviously you and I will not enjoy the Spirit's prompting or peace if we are guilty of unrepentant sin, if we continue to pause indefinitely on spiritual plateaus, or if we persist in living well beneath our spiritual privileges. My impression is that all of us understand this. What we do not so readily understand is that the power of the Holy Ghost may come and go, in terms of its intensity and evident involvement in our lives. What President Harold B. Lee taught about testimony is true with respect to the work of the Comforter. He explained that our testimony today will not be our testimony tomorrow: "Testimony is as elusive as a moonbeam; it's as fragile as an orchid; you have to recapture it every morning of your life."[3] In practical language, this means that we should take heart when we do not feel the presence of the Holy Ghost with the same magnitude on a regular, ongoing basis.

A few years ago I experienced something I had never undergone before—I went into a deep depression for several months. Oh, I had had a bad day here and there, had known frustration and disillusionment like everyone else, but I had never been trapped by the tentacles of clinical depression so severely that I simply could not be comforted and could not see the light at the end of the tunnel. For days at a time I only wanted to sleep or gaze at the walls or be alone. For weeks I felt as though I was in a closed casket, a prison cell that allowed no light or sound whatever.

Oh, how I prayed for deliverance. I sought for and received priesthood blessings. I counseled with friends who had known firsthand my pain and alienation. One physician described my condition as "depletion depression," a time when my body, my emotions, and my mind had chosen—whether I liked it or not—to take a vacation from normalcy.

I had been driven for too long and could no longer live on adrenaline. I clung to my wife and children. I read the Liberty Jail revelations over and over, holding tenaciously to the Lord's words: "Thine adversity and thine afflictions shall be but a small moment" (D&C 121:7). Again and again I pleaded with my Heavenly Father in the name of the Prince of Peace to lift the pall, chase the darkness away, and bring me back into the light. It was so very dark and lonely out there!

During those weeks of suffering I had great difficulty feeling the Spirit. In my head I knew that I was *worthy*, in the sense that I was striving to live in harmony with the teachings of the Savior, but I simply did not *feel* the peace and joy and divine approbation that I had come to expect and cherish. I was serving as a stake president at the time, and the First Presidency and my area presidency tenderly and kindly encouraged me to turn everything over to my counselors, take a needed break, and follow the doctor's orders, including using medication if prescribed.

Let me see if I can state this more accurately: I knew *in my mind* and *in my heart* that the Lord was pleased with my life, but I did not *feel* close to God as I had felt only days and weeks before. This experience, which passed after a few months, taught me something that is extremely valuable: It is one thing to *have* the Spirit of the Lord with us, even the constant companionship of that member of the Godhead, and another to always *feel* that influence.

Many times, if not most, when the Spirit is enlightening us, we feel it. Many times, if not most, when we are being divinely led, we are aware of it. But there are occasions when the Holy Ghost empowers our words or directs our paths and we, like the Lamanites who had been taught by Helaman's sons (Nephi and Lehi) and enjoyed a mighty spiritual rebirth, know it not (3 Nephi 9:20). That is to say, there is a mental or intellectual component to spiritual living that is in many ways just as important as the emotional component. Sometimes God tells us in our minds, sometimes in our hearts, and sometimes both (D&C 8:2–3).

As a priesthood leader, I witnessed with sheer delight the Holy Spirit return to the countenances of individuals who had been involved in serious transgression but who had repented and made changes in their bearing and their behavior. They were forgiven. Their sin was now behind them. Yet some could not let it go and could not forgive themselves. Strangely, they sought instead to respond more to some sense of personal inner justice than to the work of the Spirit and the word of their ecclesiastical leader. In many interviews in which I counseled them to "not look back" and to "move on" with their lives, I found myself reading the following profound lesson from the apostle John: "If our heart condemn us"—that is, if our overactive conscience continues to plague us after a remission of sins has been granted—"*God is greater than our heart, and knoweth all things*" (1 John 3:20; emphasis added).

Now, let's get back to where we started. Each of us, at different times in life, encounters what we might call "seasons of unrest"—periods of time when we do not feel close to the Lord, when we feel unworthy, when we feel almost as though God has turned his back on us, when we find ourselves filled with questions and perhaps even doubts. During such seasons we can learn remarkable lessons from the saintly woman who came to be known to the world simply as Mother Teresa of Calcutta. Born Gonxha Agnes Bojaxhiu in 1910 (a tough name to pronounce, to be sure), this slight but spiritually sensitive soul determined early in life that she wanted to serve her Lord and Savior through loving and caring for the "poorest of the poor" in India. In September 1928 she traveled to Ireland to become a part of the Institute of the Blessed Virgin Mary, a cloistered assembly of sisters dedicated to education.

In 1948 she received permission from her local authorities and from Rome to assume a different role as a nun, to go into the streets, to visit the homes of the poor and the starving, the sick and the dying, and to deliver tenderness, food, love, and a kindly word, including the word of salvation found in and through Jesus Christ. She had felt a specific call from God to do this in 1946.

In 1948, after Mother Teresa established the congregation (ministry) known as the Missionaries of Charity and was named its overseer (under her local bishop), her work expanded and grew to fill the earth. As a result, the poorest of the poor in many lands began to receive the comfort, peace, sustenance, and dignity to which each person is entitled as a child of God. She continued her work, driven and directed by the charity that flows from heaven, until her frail and spent body gave up the ghost in 1997. She left behind a legacy of love that will forever be celebrated.

That's the story. But let's take a moment now to speak of "the rest of the story," a poignant insight into her life that was not known by the public until the tenth anniversary of her death. In 2007, when Brian Kolodiejchuk, a member of the Missionaries of Charity, published a book titled *Mother Teresa: Come Be My Light,* he made known most of her personal correspondence.

With that correspondence, he revealed a secret she had carried in her heart for fifty years.

You see, despite a lifetime spent in the service of God and her fellow mortals, decades of taxing and arduous labor and grueling hours devoted to the refuse and offscouring of society, and almost seventy years of ministering to "the least of these" (Matthew 25:40), Mother Teresa had lived a life of pain, emptiness, spiritual alienation, doubt, and despair. The author explained that "Mother Teresa strove to be that light of God's love in the lives of those who were experiencing darkness. For her, however, the paradoxical and totally unsuspected cost of her mission was that she herself would live in "'terrible darkness.'"[4]

Mother Teresa wrote that since about 1949 or 1950 "this terrible sense of loss—this untold darkness—this loneliness, this continual longing for God—which gives me that pain deep down in my heart—Darkness is such that I really do not see—neither with my mind nor with my reason—the place of God in my soul is blank—There is no God in me—when the pain of longing is so great—I just long & long for God—and then it is that I feel—He does not want me—He is not there—. . . The torture and pain I can't explain."[5]

Her season of unrest, nearly fifty years' worth, actually caught her off guard; it was not something, in her wildest imaginations, she would have anticipated. And yet, despite it all, despite the doubt and the pain and the agony of loneliness, despite what she did not *feel*, she knew in her mind that God loved her, was reinforcing and upholding her, and would stand by her. In time she came to realize that her sufferings were divinely orchestrated by God to allow her to more closely identify with those with whom she spent her life—the lonely, the confused, the starving, the downtrodden— and to allow her to know something of their pain. With greater maturity she also came to know that her torturous personal agonies had been put in place to humble her, to drive her to her knees, to cause her to trust implicitly in the Lord Jesus Christ, and to allow her a glimpse into the nature of her Redeemer's passion, alienation, rejection, and emptiness during the hours of Gethsemane and Golgotha. She became a fellow traveler on the road of pain, one who participated in the fellowship of his suffering.[6]

Mother Teresa certainly didn't live in the light and joy and peace and solace and sweet refreshment that one would expect to be enjoyed by such a saintly person, but she possessed a faith in Jesus—a total trust, a complete confidence, and a ready reliance upon his merits, mercy, and grace—that transcended her bitter cup and gave her the unbelievable strength and enabling power to carry on her labors and maintain her optimism and tender tutorials to her sisters and co-workers. "Cheerfulness," Mother Teresa wrote, "is a sign of a generous and mortified person who, forgetting all things, even herself, tries to please her God in all she does for souls. Cheerfulness is often a cloak which hides a life of sacrifice, continual union with God, fervor, and generosity."[7]

David C. Steinmetz has written: "From time to time everyone endures a barren period in the life of faith. Prayers bounce off the ceiling unanswered. Hymns stick in one's throat, and whatever delight one once felt in the contemplation or worship of God withers away.

"In such circumstances Christians should 'do what is in them'—that is, *they should keep on keeping on.* They should keep on with their prayers, their hymns of praise and their daily round of duties. Even though it seems like they are walking through an immense and limitless desert, with oases few and far between, they plod on, *knowing that obedience is more important than emotional satisfaction and a right spirit than a merry heart.*

"To such people, 'God does not deny grace.' They live in hope, however, that sooner or later the band will strike up a polka and the laughter and the dancing will start all over again. But if it does not—and it did not in Mother Teresa's case—the grace that was in the beginning will be at the end as well. Of that, one can be sure. . . .

" . . . *She did not abandon the God who seemed to have abandoned her, as she very well might have done. By doubting vigorously but not surrendering to her doubts, she became a witness to a faith that did not fail and a hidden God who did not let her go.* That is what sanctity is all about."[8]

It almost seems anticlimactic to speak at this juncture of my own meager problems when I consider those through which Mother Teresa was called upon to pass. But I would say this: I still have my moments and days of depression that creep into my soul unexpectedly, times when I feel confined and shrouded and gloomy and overwhelmed. But I have learned to work through them—to keep on keeping on. And yes, there are those times when questions arise, hard questions—whether challenges to our doctrine or instances in the history of the Church—when I am stumped for a season or baffled for a time. But I will not give in to doubt or fear. I know what I know, and I refuse to discard or belittle what I know because of some miniscule matter that my limited understanding cannot explain for the time being.

Elder Orson Pratt explained that if a person received direct heavenly guidance in every aspect of his life, "where would be his trials? This would lead us to ask, Is it not absolutely necessary that God should in some measure, withhold even from those who walk before him in purity and integrity, a portion of his Spirit, that they may prove to themselves, their families and neighbors, and to the heavens whether they are full of integrity even in times when they have not so much of the Spirit to guide and influence them? I think that this is really necessary, consequently I do not know that we have any reason to complain of the darkness which occasionally hovers over the mind."[9]

Similarly, Elder Richard G. Scott stated that we should take heart when no answer comes after extended prayer. "Be thankful that sometimes God lets you struggle for a long time before that answer comes. Your character will grow; your faith will increase. . . .

". . . You may want to express thanks when that occurs, for it is an evidence of His trust."[10] In short, said Elder Robert D. Hales, "Revelation comes on the Lord's timetable, which often means we must move forward in faith, even though we haven't received all the answers we desire."[11]

On many occasions the Spirit of the living God has whispered truth to my heart, verities that my head did not yet comprehend. But I have learned to wait. Far too many manifestations of divine favor and confirmations of the truth concerning scores of matters—coming through the Spirit and founded upon the rock of revelation—have come into my mind and heart for me to trip over the pebbles of what I do not yet know. I will be patient. The Almighty has spoken in words and feelings that I cannot and dare not deny. My soul is at rest.

5

LEANING ON OTHERS

None of us can face life—its ironies and surprises, its challenges and barricades, its tragedies and traumas—on our own. Nor should we be expected to do so. A belief in the brotherhood and sisterhood of all men and women follows naturally from a belief that God is the Father of the human race. In many ways we are all in this together, and our common humanity runs much deeper than our similarities or differences in race, color, or creed.

If God had his way, no person would be left alone. If God had his way, no woman would be deserted by a man who chose not to keep his covenants. If God had his way, no children would be shuffled off to a social services agency because their mother and father could not free themselves from addictions. And if God had his way, no elderly man or woman would be deserted in an assisted living residence without regular and happy visits from sons and daughters, grandchildren, and friends. We are meant to live in community. The highest form of community on earth, the Zion of our God—made up of people who are "pure in heart" (D&C 97:21)—is a place where every man seeks "the interest of his neighbor" and does all things "with an eye single to the glory of God" (D&C 82:19).

When we are feeling lost, we should be able to ask directions of someone. When we are perplexed, we ought to be able to find a caring soul who can provide perspective. When we are wrestling with loneliness or despair or depression, it is comforting to know that beloved associates are close at hand to offer their heart, their empathy, and their love. Covenant disciples of Jesus Christ promise, as a part of their baptism into Christianity, to be willing to "bear one another's burdens, that they may be light; yea, and . . . willing to mourn with those that mourn; yea, and comfort those that stand in need of comfort" (Mosiah 18:8–9). In short, to join the Church of Jesus Christ, the body of Christ, is to enlist as a participant in the grand enterprise of lifting, liberating, and lightening the heavy burdens of others within the household of faith, to reach out and actually search out those who could use a helping hand or a warm heart.

Every member of Christ's Church is entitled to have questions, to come across ideas or doctrines or historical incidents that raise concerns. Similarly, every member has the right to turn to someone for assistance, to seek answers or clarification from another member of the Church. There is no shame in not having all the answers. We will spend our lives answering one question after another, and yet, when we breathe our last breath in mortality, we still will not have come to a perfect understanding.

I will be forever grateful to my gospel mentors through the years. When my family became fully active in the Church, and while my father was busy trying to learn the principles of salvation as quickly and thoroughly as he could, I turned frequently to my Uncle Joseph. He knew the gospel was true, and he knew the gospel. I have many happy memories of sitting at his home on Chippewa Street in Baton Rouge, asking one question after another, leaving a couple of hours later filled and refreshed with truth. I can remember Dad becoming a member of the LDS Book Club, receiving a new book each month in the mail, and adding it to his growing gospel library. I remember as a teenager that my cousin Linda and I chose to hang around with the old folks after Sunday family dinners and holidays, listening intently to doctrinal conversations, asking our own questions and thinking deep down, *It just doesn't get any better than this.*

I was blessed with teachers in Sunday School and priesthood meetings who were not only devoted to their calling but also well schooled in the faith—men and women whose love for the Lord shone in their countenances and whose testimonies and teachings went down into my young heart and burned like fire.

I recall several occasions spending time with the Whitney family for lunch, all of us having long discussions with Sister Margarite Whitney and sensing her excitement for the Lord, his doctrine, and his Church. Charles and Yvonne Dixon were models of faith and faithfulness to me through those formative years, and it would be impossible for me to enumerate all they taught me (she in Primary and he in Sunday School, priesthood meetings, and everywhere else). I once rode from Baton Rouge to Houston to a regional volleyball tournament with Ted Hicks, who took occasion to teach me great lessons about recognizing Satan's ploys and avoiding serious sin, lessons I can still vividly remember more than forty years later.

The Lord was good to me, and I never feared there was any issue that I could not take to my family members, Church leaders, or teachers for answers. I learned early to lean on others who knew more than I did. I still do so today.

On more than one occasion while serving as a full-time missionary, I had the privilege of hearing from Elder Harold B. Lee, one of the senior members of the Quorum of the Twelve Apostles. Elder Lee came to New York City regularly to attend board meetings, and he would often stop by the mission home, meet with my mission president, and spend time with the missionaries. At least three times I heard words to this effect from Elder Lee: "Elders and Sisters, I sense that not all of you have the kind of testimony that you would like to have. I sense that some of you are a bit hesitant to say with boldness, 'I know.' Well, let me say this: If you don't know for sure, then *you lean on my testimony, for I do know.*" I always felt something profound in his simple words: I knew he knew; he knew in ways I couldn't really comprehend at the time.

"Lean on me when you're not strong" are not only words that make for a memorable pop song but also a solid bit of folk wisdom when it comes to spiritual stability and faithful endurance to the end. No man is an island. We need never walk alone, for we are not alone. Further, one need not see dependence on others as a sign of weakness. It is not. In some ways, it is a sign of strength, certainly an evidence of humility. It is significant that the Savior regards this willingness to lean upon the faith of others to be a spiritual gift. "To some it is given by the Holy Ghost to know that Jesus Christ is the Son of God, and that he was crucified for the sins of the world. *To others it is given to believe on their words, that they also might have eternal life if they continue faithful*" (D&C 46:13–14; emphasis added).

That such a person can believe on the testimony of others and gain eternal life is not unimportant. As Elder Bruce R. McConkie has written: "Prophets and apostles and the elders of Israel preach the gospel and testify of Christ and his divine Sonship, *having first received the divine message by personal revelation.* Some believe their words and know in their hearts that they have heard the truth. The truths taught may be new and strange to the hearers, but *their acceptance is instinctive, automatic, without restraint;* they need hear no further arguments. The Spirit-guided words find firm lodgment in their souls by the power of the Spirit. *This ability to believe is a gift of God.*

"Individuals who have not yet advanced in spiritual things to the point of gaining for themselves personal and direct revelation from the Holy Ghost may yet have *power to believe what others, speaking by the power of the Spirit, both teach and testify.* They have power to recognize the truth of the words of others who do speak by the power of the Spirit, even though they cannot attune themselves to the Infinite so as to receive the divine word direct from heaven and without the helps of others to teach them."[1]

It was Nephi, son of Lehi, who, "having great desires to know of the mysteries of God"—those sacred verities that can only be made known by the power of the Holy Spirit—cried unto the Lord. "And behold," Nephi says, "*he did visit me, and did soften my heart that I did believe all the words which had been spoken by my father*" (1 Nephi 2:16; emphasis added).

Many of us read these words carefully and are somewhat surprised, for we would suppose Nephi to be one who already had a heart that was receptive and attentive to spiritual realities. But we are all growing, day by day, and the process of yielding our hearts unto God, educating our desires, sharpening our consciences, and enjoying more regular communion with the Infinite are lifetime pursuits, even for people as righteous and noble as Nephi. Now notice what follows in his record:

"And I spake unto Sam, making known unto him the things which the Lord had manifested unto me by his Holy Spirit. And it came to pass that he believed in my words" (1 Nephi 2:17). Sam leaned on Nephi and knew by the Spirit that what his younger brother taught was from the Lord. That decision proved to have everlastingly positive consequences.

Now I would like to contrast the sweet experiences Nephi and Sam had with a later episode in the Book of Mormon, a story not so uplifting. Concerning the time just before the conversion of Alma the Younger and the sons of Mosiah, Mormon writes that "there were many of the rising generation that could not understand the words of king Benjamin, being little children at the time he spake unto his people; and they did not believe the tradition of their fathers. They did not believe what had been said concerning the resurrection of the dead, neither did they believe concerning the coming of Christ."

Two decades had passed, and the "rising generation"—the young people—chose not to believe what their parents had felt and understood from King Benjamin's mighty sermon (Mosiah 2–4). Then follows this poignant insight from Mormon: "And now *because of their unbelief they could not understand the word of God;* and their hearts were hardened" (Mosiah 26:1–3; emphasis added).

The italicized words in this last verse are a sermon on their own. People who don't believe don't understand. People who allow their hearts to become hardened, who revel and even delight in cynicism, will forevermore fall short of what they might know and grasp, unless they repent. People who allow their questions to morph into doubts and who even delight in those doubts will never understand doctrines and principles that are beautifully simple and plain to "the weak and the simple" (D&C 1:23).

Those who have unanswered questions, who allow themselves to simmer in skepticism, and who eventually become hardened in their ignorance are generally those who choose to keep their questions to themselves, refuse to admit their need for knowledge, and decide to face their fears alone, or, instead, they turn in the wrong direction for help. Men and women who want to know more about Jesus, especially about the sacred truths he taught, the miracles he wrought, the salvation he bought, do not go to Pontius Pilate or Caiaphas for answers; they turn instead to Peter, James, or John— those who knew Jesus best.

Likewise, those who wrestle with a particular teaching or practice of Joseph Smith do not go for answers to such apostates as E. D. Howe, William E. McLellin, or William Law; instead, they go to those who knew the Prophet best, who spent hours and weeks and months and years in close company with him. Men like Brigham Young, Parley P. Pratt, and Heber C. Kimball knew best the power of his prophetic mantle and saw firsthand the depth of his purity. When we lean our ladder of faith against a wall for support, we must be sure that we do not lean it against the wrong wall.

While I worked as the director of the institute of religion adjacent to Florida State University, it was not uncommon to have students drop by all through the week to study, play Ping-Pong, share their mission calls, associate with their LDS friends, and ask me questions. More than once I had an exchange that went something like this:

Student: "Brother Millet, are you aware of such and such doctrinal or historical issue?"

Me: "Yes, I am."

Student: "Have you studied it out carefully, and do you know all the issues?"

Me: "Yes, I have, and I think I understand what troubles people about it."

Student: "Does it bother you?"

Me: "No, not at all."

Student: "Do you have an answer for the problem?"

Me: "I do. Would you like me to respond to the question?"

Student: "No, that's okay. As long as you're aware of it and have an answer for it, I'm fine."

Me: "I'd be more than happy to take the time to show you why this isn't something that should bother you, if you'd like."

Once in a great while a student might say, "Yea, let's get into it." Most seemed content that I was unruffled by the matter. They knew I knew, and for them that was enough—for the time being at least.

I have a deep and abiding testimony of this work. There is no doubt whatsoever in my mind or heart that we are engaged in the work of the Almighty and that his hand is over it. I know these things through personal revelation that has come to my soul through the power of the Holy Spirit. My witness is now independent of any other man or woman.

It was not always so, for I leaned many times upon the testimony of Uncle Joseph, Mom and Dad, the Dixons, the Whitneys, and a host of witnesses who had come to know for themselves. Theirs was a strong stabilizing influence in my life, an oasis of answers and assurance in what could have been a desert of doubt. It has been my privilege and opportunity to work closely with marvelous men and women in the Church Educational System whose witness is akin to mine. They know the gospel is true, and they know the gospel.

For that reason I have spent hundreds of hours in the offices of such dear friends as Robert Matthews,

Larry Dahl, Joseph McConkie, Andy Skinner, Brent Top, Camille Fronk Olson, Paul Peterson, Dan Judd, Cathy Thomas, Dennis Largey, and so many others I cannot list them. What was I doing? Asking questions, probing beyond what I already knew, seeking to reconcile what is unknown with what is known, and striving for both a settled mind and a soothed heart. Though my witness is independent, I have been leaning on the testimonies and talents and insights of good people for a long time. I still do. I plan to continue doing so.

Because of my work in religious education at Brigham Young University for more than a quarter century, and particularly during the decade I served as dean, it has also been my privilege to come to know many of the general Church leaders and to feel the power of their apostolic testimonies. It is clear beyond dispute that they know, they know they know, and that awareness provides a confidence and sweet boldness that empowers them to stand as witnesses of the name of Christ in all the world.

These are some pretty impressive men who are bright and brilliant and energetic and quick—men who could be utilizing their education or training to lead major corporations, preside over colleges and universities, be intimately involved in forwarding scientific innovations, serving in federal or national judgeships, and so forth. And yet they have put aside worldly pursuits and aspirations in response to a call from a prophet—a call that they sensed, and regularly testify, came from God.

Are we to suppose they have all been duped? Hypnotized? Brainwashed? Pressured in some way to assume a role that demands a completely consecrated life? Hardly! Even though I have a witness of my own, even though my conviction lies deep within the inner recesses of my soul, I still lean upon these great men—prophets, seers, and revelators. I look to them, I listen to them, I love them, and I study and cross-reference their words into my scriptures.

Jesus is my Lord and Savior, and my worship is reserved for him, but these men are like Matthew, Thomas, James, and Bartholomew in the first century—they are the chosen and ordained servants of the Lord Jesus, and they deserve my respect, allegiance, and trust. When I am tempted to worry and fret over some silly matter, it is not uncommon for me to ask myself: Would President Boyd K. Packer be troubled by this? Would Elder Dallin H. Oaks be bothered? Would Elder Jeffrey R. Holland wring his hands in despair?

Because the Spirit has borne witness to me that they are exactly what and whom we sustain and uphold them to be, I take comfort in their assurance. I rest easy because they refuse to take counsel from their fears. I am at peace because they are at peace.

At this point, we need to address an obvious question: "Yes, but shouldn't the day come when I gradually lean on others less and stand boldly on my own?" Well, of course. We cannot pause on spiritual plateaus for too long.[2] The purpose of the gospel—the cleansing and enabling power of the Atonement, working through the Holy Spirit—is not just to make bad men good and good men better, although it does do that. The gospel is the power of God unto salvation (Romans 1:16), the power by which dead men and women are brought to life, both spiritually and physically. It is the power by which testimony comes, hope is established, and sweet assurance settles upon the mind and heart like the dews from heaven.

President Heber C. Kimball reminded us that the Church has many tight places through which to pass in our quest for celestial glory, and it will require a people who are convinced and committed to what they are doing. He added that "a *test*, a TEST, a TEST [is] coming." The time would come, President Kimball said, when no man or woman would be able to survive the test of the day on borrowed light; all would be required to be guided by the light within them. Otherwise, they would not be able to stand.[3]

Of course each of us desires to "grow up unto the Lord" (Helaman 3:21). Each of us desires to mature in the things of righteousness until we receive "a fulness of the Holy Ghost" (D&C 109:15). We love and treasure the associations and examples of friends and family and Church leaders, but we must eventually be weaned, at least to some extent, from their testimony so that we can stand on our own. As the Savior declared, "Therefore, let every man stand or fall, by himself, and not for another; or not trusting another" (JST, Mark 9:44).

I sat in the solemn assembly in the Tabernacle in Salt Lake City when President Harold B. Lee was sustained as the eleventh president of The Church of Jesus Christ of Latter-day Saints. After the sustaining of Church officers was completed, President Lee spoke to the assembly and delivered one of the greatest, most moving and motivating sermons I have ever heard. The room seemed to be aflame with the Spirit of God. Following his remarks, the newly sustained member of the Quorum of the Twelve was called upon to speak.

In his opening remarks, Elder McConkie said: "As members of the church and kingdom of God on earth, we enjoy the gifts of the Spirit—those wonders and glories and miracles that a gracious and benevolent God always has bestowed upon his faithful saints. The first of these gifts listed in our modern revelation on spiritual gifts is the gift of testimony, the gift of revelation, the gift of knowing of the truth and divinity of the work. This gift is elsewhere described as the testimony of Jesus, which is the spirit of prophecy. *This is my gift. I know this work is true.*

"*I have a perfect knowledge that Jesus Christ is the Son of the living God and that he was crucified for the sins of the world.* I know that Joseph Smith is a prophet of God through whose instrumentality the fullness of the everlasting gospel has been restored again in our day. And I know that this Church of Jesus Christ of Latter-day Saints is the kingdom of God on earth, and that as now constituted, . . . it has the approval and approbation of the Lord, is in the line of its duty, and is preparing a people for the second coming of the Son of Man."[4]

It is impossible for me to describe what I felt at that moment. The occasion was spiritually electrifying. It was as though I had been invited to enter the realm of divine experience, glance with the speaker upon the scenes of eternity, and come to know for myself what he knew. To be sure, I knew he knew, and I knew he knew in ways that I did not know. I have never fully recovered from that day, for there have been few times that I have knelt in prayer since then, now almost four decades later, that I have not pleaded with a gracious God to grant unto me a testimony that is unshakable, unwavering, and undeniable.

Thirteen years later that same apostle stood at that same pulpit and bore witness in a way that shook the earth and seized the hearts of every attentive person in the Tabernacle, every sensitive person viewing or listening to the proceedings, and every receptive person since then who has heard his closing testimony to the world:

"And now, as pertaining to this perfect atonement, wrought by the shedding of the blood of God—I testify that it took place in Gethsemane and at Golgotha, and as pertaining to Jesus Christ, I testify that he is the Son of the Living God and was crucified for the sins of the world. He is our Lord, our God, and our King. *This I know of myself independent of any other person.*

"I am one of his witnesses, and in a coming day I shall feel the nail marks in his hands and in his feet and shall wet his feet with my tears.

"But *I shall not know any better then than I know now* that he is God's Almighty Son, that he is our Savior and Redeemer, and that salvation comes in and through his atoning blood and in no other way."[5]

I am not an apostle, so it is not given to me to bear apostolic witness. But the gospel has been restored in order that every man or woman might speak in the name of God the Lord (D&C 1:20). The apostles and prophets stand as examples, as models of the witness that all of us, as Saints of the Most High, should seek with all our hearts.[6] What a difference it would make in the world, what a difference it would make in discerning and detecting the evils that plague our society, and what a difference it would make if every follower of Christ knew, with unshaken faith, of the divine Sonship of their Master and trusted in his mighty arm in the fight for right!

I want you to know that I know, without question. I want my wife and children and grandchildren to know that I know. I want those who know me to feel the power of my words, observe the light of eternal truth in my countenance, and witness the effect of Christianity in my behavior and speech. I want them to know that if they do not know now, they are welcome to lean upon my testimony and my assurance, for I do know. God is my witness.

6

~⁓

USING THE SHELF

Earlier I spoke of my friend, Mr. Brown, who loved the Church and wanted his family to be a part of it but who waited patiently and painfully until he had received an inner witness of the truthfulness of the prophetic call of Joseph Smith. Some may ask, appropriately, "Why would such a good man, a sincere and honest truth seeker, be expected to wait so long?"

Let me respond boldly and quickly: I don't know. While I have been striving all of my adult life to live worthy of the influence of the Holy Ghost, I must admit that there are many things about the workings of that sacred power and influence I do not understand, including the matter of timing.

One of my colleagues, Dale LeBaron, spent hundreds of hours interviewing African Saints about their conversion to the Church. One of the questions he asked all six hundred Saints was, "When did you first sense or know that the message of the restored gospel was true?" Dale explained to me something that is sobering yet exciting. He said more than 90 percent of the people responded something like this: "The moment I heard the name Joseph Smith spoken at my door." So sudden. So immediate. And yet Brother Brown needed to wait eight years.

Some things we know for sure:

- God, our Father in Heaven, knows and loves each of his children.
- God wants each of us to come to a knowledge of the truth.
- God will do all within his power to orchestrate the events in our lives to bring us to a point of decision.
- We do not know all things, nor *can* we know all things right now.
- The knowledge of spiritual things is best taught and learned "line upon line, precept upon precept, here a little and there a little" (2 Nephi 28:30; see Isaiah 28:10).

- Answers to our questions and an understanding regarding sacred matters will come to us "in his own time, . . . and according to his own will" (D&C 88:68).
- God knows best our bearing capacity and when we are prepared to receive light and truth. Having faith in God entails having confidence in his timetable.

Let me share with you how I deal with tough questions. I search, ask those whom I respect and admire, pray for divine guidance (and sometimes add fasting to that prayer), and then reach the point that I have either resolved the dilemma, solved a portion of it, or am no closer to a resolution than when I started. I then ask myself some pertinent questions:

How much time *should* I devote to this issue? How much does it deserve? How important is this matter? Does it really make a difference? What is at stake if I do not come to an answer immediately, soon, or within the foreseeable future? Does this question, that which I do *not* know, affect what I *do* know for sure? Am I comfortable chipping away at an answer, working at it here and there as I have time?

The one thing I have learned through the years is not to become preoccupied with unanswered questions, not to obsess over them, not to allow them to make me spiritually dysfunctional. My energy and time and effort are far more importantly utilized in dealing with what I do know than in wrestling and fretting over what I do not know. In other words, I have learned to place many items *on the shelf* for the time being to allow time and study and seasoning and maturity either to prepare me for an answer down the road or to prepare me not to receive an answer, perhaps even in this life. I believe this is what it means to exercise faith in the plans and purposes of God, namely, to "hope for things which are not seen which are true" (Alma 32:21).

We must not allow ourselves to be drawn into a mental posture akin to that of anti-Christs. As noted earlier, both Sherem (Jacob 7) and Korihor (Alma 30) were prone to overgeneralize, declaring that because they did not know, no one could know. What a bold and audacious presumption! And yet, we would be wise not to allow ourselves to slide down a similar slope—to suppose that because we do not understand a matter, because we do not have an answer to our question, because we cannot reconcile A with B, then no one else can either. That's foolish. It's also terribly proud. It's like saying, "If I don't understand this, no one else on earth does either."

Putting things on the shelf is a practice that is really quite old. Adam and Eve were cast out of the Garden of Eden after they had partaken of the fruit of the tree of knowledge of good and evil. Before leaving the garden, however, they were instructed to "offer the firstlings of their flocks, for an offering unto the Lord" (Moses 5:5). Why? What was the purpose? What possible social or religious function could such a messy ritual serve?

The scriptural account states merely that "Adam was obedient unto the commandments of the Lord. And after many days an angel of the Lord appeared unto Adam, saying: Why dost thou offer sacrifices unto the Lord? And Adam said unto him: I know not, save the Lord commanded me" (Moses 5:5–6). I would suggest that the action of our first parents here was anything but blind obedience. They had walked and talked with God in the garden, knew his voice even after their expulsion from Eden, and retained in their memory a knowledge of their close association with their Heavenly Father before the Fall.[1] They knew God, and they had chosen to obey him.

They obeyed, but they were not certain why they were doing what they were doing. They chose to exercise faith. "Whatever God requires is right," the Prophet Joseph Smith said, "no matter what it is, although we may not see the reason thereof till long after the events transpire."[2] For Adam and Eve the answer eventually came: "This thing is a similitude of the sacrifice of the Only Begotten of the Father," an angel explained, "which is full of grace and truth. Wherefore, thou shalt do all that thou doest in the name of the Son, and thou shalt repent and call upon God in the name of the Son forevermore" (Moses 5:7–8).

In a sense, young Joseph Smith was required to put things on a shelf from the spring of 1820 to September 21, 1823. Between the time of the coming of the Father and the Son in the Sacred Grove until Moroni appeared at his bedside, Joseph certainly wondered about, had questions about, and wrestled with many things. For example, he was told not to join any church, but what *was* he to do religiously or spiritually?

When Brigham Young first encountered what we know as the vision of the degrees of glory (D&C 76), he had a stunningly difficult time accepting and grasping it. He had been brought up in a Protestant home, had been schooled in the tenets of traditional Christianity, and thus held to a simple notion of heaven or hell hereafter. Brother Brigham explained, "After all, my traditions were such, that when the Vision came first to me, it was directly contrary and opposed to my former education. I said, *Wait a little. I did not reject it; but I could not understand it.*"[3] At another time he declared:

"When God revealed to Joseph Smith and Sidney Rigdon that there was a place prepared for all, according to the light they had received and their rejection of evil and practice of good, it was a great trial to many, and some apostatized because God was not going to send to everlasting punishment heathens and infants, but had a place of salvation, in due time, for all, and would bless the honest and virtuous and truthful, whether they ever belonged to any church or not. It was a new doctrine to this generation, and many stumbled at it, but Joseph continued to receive revelation upon revelation, ordinance upon ordinance, truth upon truth, until he obtained all that was necessary for the salvation of the human family."[4]

President Joseph F. Smith said: "When I as a boy first started out in the ministry, I would frequently go out and ask the Lord to show me some marvelous thing, in order that I might receive a testimony. But *the Lord withheld marvels from me, and showed me the truth, line upon line,* precept upon precept, here a little and there a little, *until he made me to know the truth from the crown of my head to the soles of my feet, and until doubt and fear had been absolutely purged from me.* He did not have to send an angel from the heavens to do this. . . . By the whisperings of the still small voice of the Spirit of the living God, he gave to me the testimony I possess. And by this principle and power he will give to all the children of men a knowledge of the truth that will stay with them, and it will make them to know the truth, as God knows it, and to do the will of the Father as Christ does it."[5]

Elder Robert D. Hales related: "When President David O. McKay was a young man herding cattle, he sought a witness, but it did not come until many years later while serving his mission in Scotland. He wrote, 'It was a manifestation for which as a doubting youth I had secretly prayed . . . on hillside and in meadow. It was an assurance to me that sincere prayer is answered "sometime, somewhere."'" Elder Hales then added: "The answer may be 'Not now—be patient and wait.'"[6]

Putting hard questions on the shelf is not a way of escaping. It is not burying our heads in the sand and pretending there is no problem. It is not living in a form of spiritual denial. Rather, it is an acknowledgment that God's ways are not our ways and that his thoughts are not our thoughts (Isaiah 55:8–9). It is an act of tender surrender to "believe in God; believe that he is, and that he created all things, both in heaven and in earth; believe that he has all wisdom, and all power, both in heaven and in earth; believe that man doth not comprehend all the things which the Lord can comprehend" (Mosiah 4:9).

It is to sing the hymn of praise to the Almighty with the apostle Paul: "O the depth of the riches both of the wisdom and knowledge of God! how unsearchable are his judgments, and his ways past finding out! For who hath known the mind of the Lord? or who hath been his counsellor?" (Romans 11:33–34). To put things on the shelf is to exercise spiritual discipline, to show divine restraint. It is to refuse to throw the baby out with the bathwater. It is to affirm what we believe and to admit that there are, for the time being, some things that do not make sense, that do not add up, and that need further work.

Some years ago my family and I moved from a part of the country we had come to love dearly. I was asked to assume a new assignment in the Church Educational System that required a relocation. We had been in our new home for only a few weeks when I received a telephone call late one Sunday evening. The woman on the other end of the line was deeply distraught.

"Brother Millet," she said, "this is Sister Johnson."

"Yes, Sister Johnson," I responded. "How are you and the family?"

I had known the Johnson family quite well. Brother Johnson had been a member of the bishopric in the ward we had just left (Sister Johnson had served in the presidencies of both the Primary and Relief Society), while I had served as a member of the stake presidency in that area. I knew them to be one of the most settled and secure Latter-day Saint families anywhere. They had joined the Church after having been found and taught by the missionaries ten years earlier. They were extremely missionary-minded and had been instrumental in leading several families to baptism. But there was obvious pain in Sister Johnson's voice. I tried to be positive.

"What can I do for you?"

"I desperately need your help," she said. "My husband is about to leave the Church."

Her statement nearly took away my breath.

"Leave the Church?" I asked. "What do you mean?"

She went on to explain that her husband's brother, who was not a member of the Church and who had opposed their baptism, had for several months been sending rather bitter anti-Mormon propaganda through the mail. She mentioned that at first her husband had ignored it, but after a few weeks he began perusing it out of sheer curiosity.

"I began to notice a gradual change in Bill," she stated. She pointed out that he became argumentative and uncooperative at Church, touchy and ill at ease at home, and just plain unsettled in his demeanor. "He has many questions, Brother Millet," she added, "and

I'm afraid if he doesn't get them answered pretty soon we'll lose him."

"How can I help?" I inquired.

"He wants to talk with you," Sister Johnson answered.

"Good," I said, "put him on the line."

"Oh, no," she said, "he wants to meet with you in person."

I expressed to her that such a meeting would be perfectly fine with me, but that we were now ten or twelve hours' driving distance from one another. I suggested that if this was the only way to deal with his concerns, if his concerns could not be addressed by someone in their area, then we should set a time when we might get together.

"He's already on his way," she said. "He left a couple of hours ago. Would you please meet with him? He'll be at the institute by 9 A.M."

I was somewhat startled but quickly assured Sister Johnson that I would be more than happy to meet with him and do what I could. Brother Johnson wasn't the only one who didn't sleep that night. I tossed and turned through the night, arose several times, and retired to the living room to pray for guidance. The morning came faster than I had wished, and my stomach churned as I contemplated what the meeting might entail.

Sister Johnson was quite accurate in her prediction: her husband arrived a little after nine o'clock. She was also quite accurate in her description of her husband's condition. He had a fallen countenance, a dark look in his eyes, and in general a rather gloomy appearance; this simply was not the man I had known before. He was void of the Spirit and was in many ways a broken man—like a person who had lost his way. We knelt and prayed together, and I pleaded with the Lord to dispel the spirit of gloom and doubt and endow us with the spirit of light and understanding. The answer to that prayer came eventually but only after a long and difficult struggle.

As is so often the case, Brother Johnson had been confronted with scores of questions on authority, on the Church's claim to being Christian, on temple rites, on doctrinal teachings of specific Church leaders, on changes in scripture or Church practice, and so forth. I took the time to respond to every issue and to suggest an answer if such was possible. In some cases, the answer was simply a call for faith, an invitation to pray or pray again about whether Joseph Smith was a prophet of God, about whether his successors have worn the same mantle of authority, and about whether the Church is divinely led today. I sensed, however, that there was something deeper, something beneath the surface that was being reflected in his questions, something festering and eating away at his soul like a cancer. It took me almost eight hours to discover what that something was.

When Brother and Sister Johnson were taught the gospel and introduced to the Book of Mormon, one of the missionaries—no doubt well-meaning but shortsighted—had said something like this: "Now, Brother and Sister Johnson, the Book of Mormon is true. It came from God to Joseph Smith. And you can know for yourselves that it is true by praying about it. But, the fact is, there are so many archaeological evidences of its truthfulness, these days it almost isn't necessary to pray about it!" The statement sounded convincing enough. Brother Johnson bought into that line of reasoning and—shortsighted on his part—never took occasion to pray with real intent about the Book of Mormon.

When anti-Mormon materials suggested that there were not as many current external evidences of the Nephite or Jaredite civilizations as he had been told previously, his whole world collapsed. If the Book of Mormon wasn't true, he reasoned, then Joseph Smith was not a prophet. If Joseph Smith was not a prophet, then . . .

One fatal step had led to another. And now Brother Johnson was ready to throw it all away, unfortunately, because his testimony was not substantive, his doctrinal foundation weak and shifting. And he had been unwilling to exercise sufficient faith and patience to resee and refocus upon the things that really count—in this case the message or content of the Book of Mormon.

It was almost a relief to finally get down to the core issue. I explained to him that we were now up against the wall of faith and that the only issue to be decided was whether he was willing to pay the price to know the truth. I asked some hard questions: "Did you ever know that this work is true? What was your witness based on? What has this doubting and vexation of the soul done to your wife and children? Does the bitter spirit you have felt during the past few months come from God? Are you willing to throw it all away, to jettison all that is good and ennobling because your foundation was deficient?"

He paused and reflected again with me on the painful and poignant struggling he had undergone. Then he added that he wanted more than anything to feel once more what he had felt ten years earlier.

I stressed to him the need to stay with simple and solid doctrinal matters, particularly regarding the Book of Mormon and the Restoration, to focus upon the things of greatest worth, and to follow the same course of study and pondering and prayer that he had followed during his initial investigation of the Church. I challenged him to never yield to the temptation to quit the Church when he encountered things he didn't understand, especially when there were so many things he *did* understand and know. It was a sweet experience to watch the light of faith and trust come back into his countenance and his life.

This experience highlights the tragic reality that people are often prone to jump ship, forsake family and friends and faith, and give it all up because they face an unanswered question, an unresolved dilemma, or a new development in life that defies explanation. They refuse to put something on the shelf until more insight is forthcoming.

Each of us is under obligation to search and ponder issues ourselves and to do our best to learn by study and by faith the answers to our concerns (D&C 9:7–9; 88:118). Every member of the Church has a direct channel to our Heavenly Father. While Jesus is our Mediator and our Intercessor, we have been counseled to "come boldly unto the throne of grace, that we may obtain mercy, and find grace to help in time of need" (Hebrews 4:16). Each of us who enjoys the companionship and guidance of the Holy Spirit—the Comforter, even that Spirit of Truth that knows all things (D&C

42:17; Moses 6:61)—can go to God in prayer, express feelings, pose questions, and seek for inspiration.

In addition, members of a given ward can readily take their concerns to their priesthood leaders—their branch president or bishop. If a leader does not know the answer to a question, he can inquire of the stake president. If the stake president is unable to address the concern and feels it advisable to do so, he may inquire of the general authorities of the Church.

As indicated earlier, people ought to feel free to ask their questions. If an answer is to be had, it can be obtained through proper channels. When we are troubled by a particular matter, we may be tempted to spend an inordinate amount of time researching it. Some things have just not been revealed, so to devote ourselves endlessly to the discovery of what in essence is the undiscoverable (at least for now) is counterproductive. It's almost a waste of time, especially when our efforts could be so much more profitably expended by studying and reinforcing our testimony of the things God *has* revealed.

We reduce the realm of the unknown not by wandering in it but rather by delighting in and expanding our knowledge of that which God has already revealed. It is a soul-satisfying experience to be reading topic A and then to have our minds caught away to consider topic B. Indeed, serious, consistent, prayerful consideration and reflection upon the *institutional* revelations (the standard works and the words of the living oracles) result in *individual* revelations, including—where the Lord senses it is appropriate and we are ready to receive it—the answers to our more difficult questions. Those answers may come as a specific response to a specific concern, or they may come in the form of a comforting and peaceful assurance that all is well, that God is in his heaven, that the work in which we are engaged is true, that specifics will be made known in the Lord's due time. Answers do come but only when we go to the right source.

Let me say simply that I know that God answers prayers, that he wants us to be calm and settled about our faith, that he desires that we turn to him for direction and perspective, and that those answers come through a scriptural discovery, a doctrinal discussion, a sermon or gospel lesson, the dreams of the night, or the whisperings of the still, small voice. Many of the answers I have sought have come rather quickly; in other cases, my questions have remained on the shelf for many years. My faith, however, is such that I know, beyond all doubt, that sooner or later my mind and my heart will be settled and soothed regarding those things now withheld from me.

A related tendency by some is to parade their doubts and to suppose that by coming out of the closet with an announcement of all things that trouble them, they will somehow either feel better about their difficulties or identify and join hands with others who similarly struggle. As suggested already, we need not suffer alone. There is help available within fairly easy reach. Precious little good comes, however, from hanging out our dirty laundry by making public proclamations about our inner anxieties. Such behavior merely feeds doubt and perpetuates it.

Elder Neal A. Maxwell asked, "Why are a few members, who somewhat resemble the ancient Athenians, so eager to hear some new doubt or criticism? (See Acts 17:21). Just as some weak members slip across a state line to gamble, a few go out of their way to have their doubts titillated. Instead of nourishing their faith, they are gambling 'offshore' with their fragile faith. To the question, 'Will ye also go away?' [John 6:67] these few would reply, 'Oh, no, we merely want a weekend pass in order to go to a casino for critics or a clubhouse for cloakholders.' Such easily diverted members are not disciples but fair-weather followers.

"Instead, true disciples are rightly described as steadfast and immovable, pressing forward with 'a perfect brightness of hope.' (2 Ne. 31:20; see also D&C 49:23)."[7]

We have only so much time and energy in this life; we would do well to ignore, where possible, the unimportant, and to avoid getting caught up, as someone has suggested, in the thick of thin things! As a professor of religion at Brigham Young University for almost thirty years, I have found it fascinating (and sometimes a bit discouraging) to see what some students grapple with. This one just has to know the exact size of Kolob. That one won't rest until he has calculated the precise dimensions of the celestial city seen by John the Revelator. Others wrestle with the present resting place of the ark of the covenant or Joseph Smith's seer stone.

"There is so much to learn," Elder Bruce R. McConkie has written, "about the great eternal verities which shape our destiny that it seems a shame to turn our attention everlastingly to the minutiae and insignificant things. So often questions like this are asked: 'I know it is not essential to my salvation, but I would really like to know how many angels can dance on the head of a pin and if it makes any difference whether the pin is made of brass or bronze?' There is such a thing as getting so tied up with little fly specks on the great canvas which depicts the whole plan of salvation that we lose sight of what the life and the light and the glory of eternal reward are all about. (See Matthew 23:23–25.) There is such a thing as virtually useless knowledge, the acquisition of which won't make one iota of difference to the destiny of the kingdom or the salvation of its subjects."[8]

In teaching some of my religion classes, I have occasionally said that it is as important to know what we *do not know* as it is to know what *we do know*. Further, to quarrel and dispute over the unknown and the unrevealed is fruitless and absolutely unnecessary. In that spirit, it is fundamentally necessary for us occasionally to say, "I don't know!" Part of our spiritual maturity is reflected in our ability to deal with ambiguity, to handle uncertainty. And yet our focus need not be upon the unknown; rather, we can emphasize what we *do* know. This is the pattern found in scripture, the pattern whereby a prophet says, in essence, "I don't know this, but let me tell you what I do know." An angel asked Nephi, "Knowest thou the condescension of God?" Note the young prophet's response: "I know that he loveth his children; nevertheless, I do not know the meaning of all things" (1 Nephi 11:16–17; compare Alma 7:8; 40:8–9).

We continue our searching, our prayer, our discussions, but we wait patiently upon the Lord. I, like many others, do not understand for the present all the things that took place in the history of the restored Church or all the doctrines preached by leaders of the Church. But my confidence and my trust in Joseph Smith and his successors is implicit. We simply do not have the whole story yet. We must be patient, avoiding the temptation to attribute improper motivation or to jump prematurely to conclusions. We need to give the leaders of the Church the benefit of the doubt. The Lord will vindicate the words and works of his anointed servants in time. Of this I have no doubt.

I have placed many things on a shelf during the past thirty years. A number of those items have come down from the shelf as information and inspiration have replaced darkness and uncertainty with light and understanding. I have also placed some new items on the shelf. Placing and removing them is part of our spiritual maturity and growth. Some matters will probably stay on the shelf until that glorious millennial day when God makes known those things "which have passed, and hidden things which no man knew, things of the earth, by which it was made, and the purpose and the end thereof—things most precious, things that are above, and things that are beneath, things that are in the earth, and upon the earth, and in heaven" (D&C 101:33–34).

Joseph Smith wrote that "the things of God are of deep import; and time, and experience, and careful and ponderous and solemn thoughts can only find them out."[9] If we will submit to God, surrender our will to him, and trust in his plan and timetable, we will come to know, in the midst of our earthly challenges, the peace that passes all understanding (Philippians 4:7). If we are able to say, with Job, "Though [God] slay me, yet will I trust in him" (Job 13:15), the shroud of doubt and spiritual darkness will be lifted and removed by the winds of faith and trust in our Redeemer. We will then begin to see things as they really are.

7

DOUBTING OUR DOUBTS

I don't think I have ever met a person who chose to leave The Church of Jesus Christ of Latter-day Saints and then cited prayer and divine direction as the reason for doing so. I have no doubt that someone out there claims to have had such an experience; I just haven't met that person yet. We would never feel comfortable with a person being baptized into the Church who had not prayed and received a personal spiritual witness from the Father that this work is true. It's not enough that Latter-day Saint doctrine makes good sense, is intellectually sound, and fits together well.

While Mormonism certainly has an intellectual component to it that makes it attractive, conversion to the faith and entrance into the Church ought to take place because investigators come to know for themselves following sincere and earnest prayer and by the power of the Holy Spirit. People who come into the Church through witnessing a miracle or who are baptized as a result of some extraordinary event are people who need to be watched over carefully and nurtured by priesthood leaders, home and visiting teachers, and ward or branch members. We come to know the things of God only by the power of the Spirit of God (1 Corinthians 2:11–14). We come to know as Alma the Younger came to know—not because we are struck down by an angel but because we engage in a process of fasting, praying, and receiving the spirit of prophecy and revelation (Alma 5:45–47).

"It is not by marvelous manifestations unto us," President Joseph F. Smith observed, "that we shall be established in the truth, but it is by humility and faithful obedience to the commandments and laws of God."[1]

Again, few people choose to change faiths or leave all faith behind as a result of a revelation from God. Rather, one unanswered question leads to another and another, followed by a period of festering and plaguing doubts, followed in turn by resignation and surrender to ignorance of, or confusion concerning, a certain matter. In other words, personal apostasy is inevitably a product of talking ourselves out of the faith—a matter of the heart losing the argument with the mind. To do so, we must reconstrue our past and mentally restructure our present. That is, we find it necessary to question what we once knew by personal revelation, to rationalize away spiritual experiences, and to quench the Spirit or ignore the inner light that once burned brightly.

Leaving the faith or choosing not to affiliate with Church members is a mental decision, a resolution that requires us to pretend that we never really felt the promptings of the Holy Ghost, that we never knew the warm and calming assurance that we were just where the Lord wanted us to be, that the distinctive message of the restored gospel—precious understanding concerning some of the deepest and most profound issues of life—no longer holds an attraction. Consider the following questions, for example:

- Who am I?
- Where did I come from?
- Why am I here?
- What will become of me after death?
- Has God spoken anew in our day through prophets?
- Have I heard or felt the spirit of revelation?

- Is what I experienced at the time of my baptism or endowment or temple marriage real?
- Have I felt the power of the Atonement in my life—enjoyed a remission of sins and experienced an infusion of the Savior's divine enabling power?
- Is what I have felt, thought, and experienced as I read the Book of Mormon, Doctrine and Covenants, Pearl of Great Price, and addresses of living apostles and prophets from God?
- Have I witnessed the power of the priesthood in my life?
- Is the doctrine that families can be together forever genuine?
- Is the hope that has burned within my soul for so long, the hope of eternal life and exaltation, true?
- Am I prepared to throw it all away and denounce what was once more powerful than sight?

It's a painful task to decide that leaving the fold is what I most desire, that my life for so many years was a major detour from truth. My recommendation to someone wavering in testimony is to expend the same time and effort to rekindle the flame of faith as was spent in gaining a witness in the first place. If you once came to know the message is true by the power of the Spirit, have you spent as much time on your knees recently, in the spirit of fasting, as you did then? Have you been direct, specific, and earnest in your pleadings to God? Do your spiritual efforts match your mental gymnastics? If it's fair game to question what you once knew to be true, it's more than fair to question your questioning.

For example, suppose I am troubled and prone to doubt the reality of the First Vision when I discover that there is more than one dictated account and that there are small variations among those accounts. Am I ready to doubt the reality of the resurrection of Jesus because the differing accounts in the four Gospels are inconsistent on how many angels appeared at the tomb? Am I prepared to doubt the reality of the conversion of Saul of Tarsus on the road to Damascus because Acts 9, 22, and 26 provide differences in detail, such as who heard the voice and saw the light? Probably not. Why? Because it is essence, not miniscule detail, that matters.

Am I prepared to jettison the Book of Mormon when I discover that, at least for now, there is no overabundance of archaeological evidence for the Lehite colony? Then what about how searching the Book of

Mormon settles my soul, stimulates my mind, and provides a deep and profound testimony to my very being that what I am reading is a true story about actual people?

Am I in a position to conclude that plural marriage, as practiced by Joseph Smith and the early Saints, was an immoral and corrupt practice that was unauthorized by God, that Brother Joseph was a "fallen prophet" as some suppose, when in fact some of the most sublime revelations, doctrines, and practices were made known through him in Nauvoo, Illinois? Could Joseph have been living in sin, void of the guiding power of the Spirit, and yet deliver to the Saints some of the most penetrating, soul-satisfying, spiritually elevating, and time-transcending truths ever given to the children of God? I don't think so.

What about when a member of the Church does something that is clearly out of bounds and well beyond propriety? Does this not raise a red flag, produce a doubt, and suggest that the restored gospel is false? Elder Boyd K. Packer offered this timely counsel:

"At times someone has come to me, their faith shaken by alleged wrongdoing of some leader in the Church. . . .

Such incidents . . . which supposedly involve Church leaders, are described as evidence that the gospel is not true, that the Church is not divinely inspired, or that it is being misled. . . .

"Have you ever, in your life, attended any Church meeting—priesthood meeting, sacrament meeting, Relief Society, Sunday School, a conference or fireside . . . where any encouragement or authorization was given to be dishonest, to cheat in business, or take advantage of anyone? . . .

"Have you read, or do you know of anything in the literature of the Church, in the scriptures themselves, in lesson manuals, in Church magazines or books, in Church publications of any kind, which contains any consent to lie, or to steal, to misrepresent, to defraud, to be immoral or vulgar, to profane, to be brutal, or to abuse any living soul? . . .

"You are active and have held positions in the Church. Surely, you would have noticed if the Church promoted any of these things in any way. . . .

"Why then . . . when you hear reports of this kind, should you feel that the Church is to blame?

"There is no provision in the teachings or doctrines of the Church for any member to be dishonest, or immoral, or irresponsible, or even careless.

"Have you not been taught all of your life, that if a member of the Church, particularly one in high position, is unworthy in any way, he acts against the standards of the Church? He is not in harmony with the teachings, the doctrines, or with the leadership of the Church.

"Why, then, should your faith be shaken by this account, or that, of some alleged misconduct—most of them misrepresented or untrue?"[2]

Not long ago I sat in my office opposite a young woman, a returned missionary, who indicated that she had decided to leave the Church to join another one to which she and her family had belonged when she was a small child. She stated rather emphatically that she had wrestled for months, since returning from her mission, with many and varied doubts, that her faith had been shaken by some anti-Mormon reading material, and that she was visiting me for one reason only—her mother had asked her to please do so.

We went through a number of questions she had, I provided an answer for each one, and I bore my testimony of the truthfulness of the restored gospel. I assured her that I too had wrestled with questions through the years but that I had made a decision a long time ago to be true to what I knew in my heart was true and to work my way through questions in a faithful manner.

I probed for quite a while to discover what her serious issues were but to no avail. I finally had the courage to ask, "We have dealt with most all of your questions, haven't we?" She nodded. "What is it, then, that is pulling you away? Why do you want to leave the Church?"

A long pause followed, accompanied by a few heavy sighs, and then she spoke these revealing words: "Okay, let me put it this way: I just don't feel like doing all the stuff the Church asks of us. You know—tithing, three-hour church meetings, scripture study, and a whole bunch of other requirements. I'm tired of doing the obedience thing. I just want to relax and enjoy life for a change." This was another matter entirely.

We then talked about the power of the Atonement to lift our spirits, lighten our burdens, and liberate us from a life of legalism—from seeing the gospel of Jesus Christ as a list of do's and don'ts and discovering that the faster we went, the more behind we found ourselves. We spoke at length about the power of the Savior to assist us to *become* and not just do and about the importance of looking to our Redeemer more than we look to the rules. We discussed not being caught up with a list of means and thereby missing the great *ends* of life— coming to know God and to feel his love and acceptance. In looking back at the interview, I realize that what I was doing was helping her to doubt her doubts, to identify the real problem, to look beneath the surface and face the facts, to engage what was truly at the foundation of her frustrations.

To doubt our doubts is to be courageous rather than cavalier when it comes to those things about which we feel some uncertainty. We cannot, for example, afford to allow ourselves to be casual in our doubting of doubts, for to do so is to yield to mental and spiritual laziness. Just as the Lord needs competent and committed disciples, so each of us should never take doubt lightly or allow a doubt to reign when in fact it has not won that lofty perch through proving itself beyond all doubt. Just as for me it takes too much faith to be an atheist—to witness, for example, the order and precision of the cosmos or the complexity of the human body and still hold to an agnostic or atheistic posture—so we should not be pushovers in allowing our faith system to go by the way without intellectual and spiritual kicking and screaming on our part.

Many are buffeted with doubt who hope against hope for a time when they can be more settled and secure in their faith. One principle to be practiced is a willful suspension of disbelief. For example, few people ever come to a reading of the Book of Mormon with a snide, skeptical, "let me prove it false" approach and then gain a witness from God that the book is true, that it is indeed another testament of Jesus Christ. Rather, to grow in faith, to come to know that which cannot come through rational processes alone, one must be willing to place doubt on the shelf and entertain an attitude of "I wonder if this might be true," or "Could this possibly be true?"

Let me put it another way. When something as serious as the salvation of my soul is at stake, I need to exert every effort to ascertain whether the matter under consideration is of the Lord or of Lucifer. If it is of the Lord, I need to know that, to know it beyond doubt. If it is of Lucifer, I need to know that also, to know it beyond doubt. Given the infinite price of a human soul, we must not cheapen the quest for truth by pretending that something is true and of God when it is not; nor must we dally with our doubts or feign disbelief, when we merely find it demanding and inconvenient to be numbered among the household of faith.

"I have actually seen a vision," Joseph Smith wrote, "and who am I that I can withstand God, or why does the world think to make me deny what I have actually seen? For I had seen a vision; I knew it, and I knew that God knew it, and I could not deny it, neither dared I do it; at least I knew that by so doing I would offend God, and come under condemnation" (Joseph Smith–History 1:25).

God knows all things, including what he has made known to us. We cannot and must not treat such knowledge lightly. Our duty as disciples is to "stir up the gift of God, which is in [us]. . . . For God hath not given us the spirit of fear; but of power, and of love, and of a sound mind. Be not thou therefore ashamed of the testimony of our Lord" (2 Timothy 1:6–8). To paraphrase Jude, the brother of Jesus, we must "earnestly contend for the faith which was once delivered" to you and me (Jude 1:3). Truly, our faith is worth fighting for.

8

RESERVOIRS OF FAITH

During those times when we seem to be swimming in uncertainty, living with ever-present questions, wondering what to do and where to go, we need to be able to draw sustenance from the reservoirs of faith within our soul. Many people who find themselves wrestling with a particular issue and feel the flame of faith flickering have discovered the worth of simply asking: What do I know for sure? What can I count on? What things could I never deny, no matter what?

I want to relate a personal experience that I have told before, this time adding details to what I have shared in the past. As a young missionary in the eastern states in 1967, I learned something about the trauma that we often feel when we are up against the wall of faith, when we want to believe but feel our grip on the iron rod slipping. My companion and I had moved into a small town in New Jersey, only to find that the local Protestant ministers had anticipated our arrival and prepared their parishioners for our coming. At almost every door we approached, we were met by a smiling face and the words, "Oh, you must be the Mormons. This is for you." They would then hand us an anti-Mormon tract.

We saved the pamphlets, stacked them in the corner of the living room of the apartment as a kind of strange souvenir, and soon had a rather substantial pile of material. Out of sheer curiosity we began to read the stuff during lunchtime. I can still recall the dark and empty feelings that filled my soul as I encountered question after question about selected doctrines and specific moments in the history of the Church. My senior companion was no different; he became as unsettled as I was.

As I recall, the booklets were not vicious or attacking so much as they attempted to demonstrate the differences between mainstream Christianity and Latter-day Saint teachings, often in a parallel column format. And, of course, what was most unsettling was the fact that the writers frequently used our own materials against us; that is, they would draw upon direct quotations from early Church leaders.

Most of the propaganda didn't trouble us at all. Some of it we actually chuckled over because the points being made were somewhat ridiculous and merely evidenced the writers' lack of understanding of LDS culture and way of life. One part in particular, however, did trouble us, for it dealt with our view of the Godhead. The writers repeatedly drew attention to what they called "inconsistency" in the way Latter-day Saint scripture and teachings referred to God, our Heavenly Father, and his Son, Jesus Christ.

We didn't chuckle much about this, for it dealt with a central and singularly important matter, namely, the God we worship. The question being raised had to do with the fact that some revelations that began in the voice of the Father ended in the voice of the Son, and vice versa. The pamphlets suggested, for example, that the language of Mosiah 15, Abinadi's commentary on Isaiah 53, was much more akin to Trinitarian teachings in traditional Christian churches than to well-accepted Latter-day Saint doctrine about God and Christ.

For weeks we did our work, but our heart wasn't in it. We went through the motions, but without saying much to each other, we sensed that we couldn't do so indefinitely. I broke the ice at lunch one afternoon with a rather brutal query: "Elder, what if the Church isn't true?" There was a long, uncomfortable pause, followed by his response: "I don't know."

I followed up: "What if the Baptists are right?" (There was a strong contingent of Baptists in the area.)

He said, "I just don't know."

Third question: "What if the Catholics are right? What if they have had the authority all along?"

His response: "I've been wondering the same thing." Then, presumably in an effort to cheer me up, he asked, "Elder Millet, do you think we are doing anything wrong? I mean, even if we are not a part of the true church, are we hurting anyone?"

I sheepishly replied that we were probably not doing anything destructive.

"Then," he added, "maybe we should keep working."

I asked with much pain in my voice, "Is that supposed to make me feel better? If so, it doesn't."

He indicated that under the present circumstances it was the best he could do. I am ashamed to admit that before this time I had never prayed intently about my testimony. I was raised in the Church. Mom and Dad had a testimony, and I knew that they knew. I had leaned upon them, as well as upon my uncle and aunt, my teachers, and my advisers. That always seemed adequate. They were good people; they wouldn't lie to me.

I knew my father to be a man of integrity, as well as a clear-headed, solid thinker. He wouldn't give his life for something that did not make sense, would he? But suddenly what they knew did not seem sufficient to settle my troubled heart.

I prayed and I pleaded. I begged the Lord for light, for truth, for help, for anything! I asked to be guided in the right direction, to be led to an answer, to solve this dilemma so that I could pour my whole heart into my work and not be weighed down with doubt. These vexations of the soul went on for some weeks. I had actually concluded (though I had not confided so to my companion) that if relief were not forthcoming shortly, I would pack my bags and go home. It did not seem proper to be engaged seriously in a cause about which I could not bear my testimony earnestly and forthrightly.

When we came home for lunch a few days later, my companion set about the task of making soup and preparing peanut butter sandwiches. I collapsed in a large chair in the living room, removed my shoes, and loosened my tie. As I began to reflect once more on my testimony problem, my heart ached. My feelings were close to the surface at this point, and I yearned for deliverance from my pain. For some reason I reached to a nearby lamp table and picked up a copy of the pamphlet, "Joseph Smith Tells His Own Story."

I began reading the opening lines. I came to the Prophet's statement that he was born on December 23, 1805, in Sharon, Windsor County, Vermont, and I was suddenly and without warning immersed in the most comforting and soothing influence I had ever known. It seemed at the time as if I were being wrapped in a large blanket as I began to be filled with the warmth of the Holy Spirit from head to toe. The spirit of conversion encompassed me, and I came to know assuredly that what we were doing was right and true and good. I did not hear specific words, but a distant voice seemed to whisper: "Of course it's true. You know that now, and you've known it for a long time."

Another feeling I had was that the answers to what was troubling me were for the time being beyond my capacity to comprehend. In time the answers would come, answers that would be as satisfying to the mind as they were soothing to the heart. I was being instructed, in other words, to put this matter on the shelf, to focus my attention elsewhere for a season, and move on. The answers came, in fact, within a matter of months when I was transferred from the area and received a new companion. He was extremely bright, articulate, and knowledgeable concerning the principles of the gospel.

I posed my question to him and supposed that he would be as mystified as I had been (there's that prideful overgeneralization I spoke of earlier). On the contrary, my new companion indicated that he had encountered these questions many times before, had done some research on the matter, and had formulated an answer based on the June 30, 1916, doctrinal exposition of the First Presidency and the Quorum of the Twelve titled "The Father and the Son." He showed me where to find the exposition in the appendix of Elder James E. Talmage's book *The Articles of Faith*. I marveled weeks later how something so simple could have been so problematic before.

The Spirit touched my heart and told me things my mind did not yet understand. I was then in a position to proceed confidently with my work until my head caught up with my heart. Formerly I was in agony, turmoil, and subject to the nagging and uncomfortable power of doubt and uncertainty. Afterward I was at peace, rest, and secure in the knowledge that my faith was well founded. I saw with new eyes and felt with a new heart.

Some people allow doubts to enter their world when they discover mistakes on the part of past Church leaders or sermons that are not in harmony with what the Church leaders proclaim today. Moses made mistakes, but we love and sustain him and accept his writings nonetheless. Peter made mistakes, but we still honor him and study his words. Paul made mistakes, but we admire his boldness and dedication, and we treasure his epistles. James pointed out that Elijah "was a man subject to like passions as we are" (James 5:17), and the Prophet Joseph Smith taught that "a prophet [is] a prophet only when he [is] acting as such."[1] On another occasion the Prophet declared, "I told them I was but a man, and they must not expect me to be perfect; if they expected perfection from me, I should expect it from them; but if they would bear with my infirmities and the infirmities of the brethren, I would likewise bear with their infirmities."[2]

One of his successors, Lorenzo Snow, said, "I can fellowship the President of the Church . . . if he does not know everything I know . . . I saw the . . . imperfections in [Joseph Smith] . . . I thanked God that He would put upon a man who had those imperfections the power and authority He placed upon him . . . for I knew that I myself had weakness, and I thought there was a chance for me."[3]

Elder Bruce R. McConkie has written, "With all their inspiration and greatness, prophets are yet mortal men with imperfections common to mankind in general. They have their opinions and prejudices and are left to work out their own problems without inspiration in many instances."[4] He added, "Thus the opinions and views, even of a prophet, may contain error, unless those opinions and views were inspired by the Spirit."[5]

In 1865 the First Presidency counseled the Latter-day Saints: "We do not wish incorrect and unsound doctrines to be handed down to posterity under the sanction of great names, to be received and valued by future generations as authentic and reliable, creating labor and difficulties for our successors to perform and contend with, which we ought not to transmit to them. The interests of posterity are, to a certain extent, in our hands. Errors in history and in doctrine, if left uncorrected by us who are conversant with the events, and who are in a position to judge of the truth or falsity of the doctrines, would go to our children as though we had sanctioned and endorsed them. . . . We know what sanctity there is always attached to the writings of men who have passed away, especially to the writings of Apostles, when none of their contemporaries are left, and we, therefore, feel the necessity of being watchful upon these points."[6]

President Gordon B. Hinckley stated, "I have worked with seven Presidents of this Church. I have recognized that all have been human. But I have never been concerned over this. They may have had some weaknesses. But this has never troubled me. I know that the God of heaven has used mortal men throughout history to accomplish His divine purposes."[7]

On another occasion President Hinckley pleaded with the Saints that "as we continue our search for truth . . . we look for strength and goodness rather than weakness and foibles in those who did so great a work in their time.

"We recognize that our forebears were human. They doubtless made mistakes. . . .

"There was only one perfect man who ever walked the earth. The Lord has used imperfect people in the process of building his perfect society. If some of them occasionally stumbled, or if their characters may have been slightly flawed in one way or another, the wonder is the greater that they accomplished so much."[8]

Some permit doubts to fester because they are not able to demonstrate, to prove physically or empirically, what they had believed so long to be true. That is, they tend to crumble or wither when they find that there are not as many archaeological evidences of the Book of Mormon as they had supposed, that some DNA studies supposedly cast doubt upon the historicity of the Book of Mormon, or that modern translations by Egyptologists of the Joseph Smith papyri or the facsimiles do not agree with the text of the book of Abraham.

Elder Neal A. Maxwell wrote: "It is the author's opinion that all the scriptures, including the Book of Mormon, will remain in the realm of faith. Science will not be able to prove or disprove holy writ. However, enough plausible evidence will come forth to prevent scoffers from having a field day, but not enough to remove the requirement of faith. Believers must be patient during such unfolding."[9]

Similarly, President Ezra Taft Benson pointed out, "We do not have to prove the Book of Mormon is true. The book is its own proof. All we need to do is read it and declare it. The Book of Mormon is not on trial— the people of the world, including the members of the Church, are on trial as to what they will do with this second witness for Christ."[10]

"It never has been the case, nor is it so now, that the studies of the learned will prove the Book or Mormon true or false. The origin, preparation, translation, and verification of the truth of the Book of Mormon have all been retained in the hands of the Lord, and the Lord makes no mistakes. You can be assured of that."[11]

President Hinckley put things in proper perspective when he taught: "I can hold [the Book of Mormon] in my hand. It is real. It has weight and substance that can be physically measured. I can open its pages and read, and it has language both beautiful and uplifting. The ancient record from which it was translated came out of the earth as a voice speaking from the dust. . . .

"The evidence for its truth, for its validity in a world that is prone to demand evidence, lies not in archaeology or anthropology, though these may be helpful to some. It lies not in word research or historical analysis, though these may be confirmatory. The evidence for its truth and validity lies within the covers of the book itself. The test of its truth lies in reading it. It is a book of God. Reasonable individuals may sincerely question its origin, but those who read it prayerfully may come to know by a power beyond their natural senses that it is true, that it contains the word of God, that it outlines saving truths of the everlasting gospel, that it came forth by the gift and power of God."[12]

Each prayer we offer, each time we fast, each charitable deed we perform, each meeting we attend, each lesson we deliver, and each testimony we bear add, bit by bit, to the reservoir of faith within our souls. In addition, every faith-building enterprise in which we engage plants a memory within the mind and heart—a sacred memory that will, if we allow it to, serve us well during moments of trial and challenge. This is one of the reasons that full-time missionaries are so effective in the work of activating men and women who once joined the Church but have since slipped into the ranks of the less active. There was a time when these people once knew by the power of the Spirit that what the missionaries taught them was true.

There was a time of quiet certitude and joy that accompanied their investigation of the Church and its teachings, a season when they loved the missionaries so very much, delighted to have them in their home, and sorrowed when they were transferred from the area. The appearance, words, and invitation of the missionaries to the less active frequently spark a sweet memory, reminding them of what they once felt and what they once accepted as true and from God. Many of these people recollect those times with fondness and often resolve to get back what they once had. It is often the case, as well, that those who left the Church under unpleasant circumstances—serious transgression or even apostasy—still feel a painful sense of loss and would confess in their hearts a desire to come back and be a part of something that is still dear to them.

During the nearly ten years I served as dean of Religious Education, I took occasion, whenever it presented itself, to visit the Sacred Grove in Palmyra, New York. During that time I visited those marvelous Church history sites at least seven or eight times. Why? Because spending time in the Sacred Grove, sitting there rereading Joseph Smith's accounts of the First Vision, and reflecting on how terribly important his vision was and is to the religious world reminded me again and again of the witness I first received and of a thousand confirming witnesses that have come to me through the years. I was being tutored and taught through the medium of memory, a significant part of my reservoir of faith.

President Spencer W. Kimball counseled us to develop reservoirs of faith "so that when the world presses in upon us, we stand firm and strong; when the temptations of a decaying world about us draw on our energies, sap our spiritual vitality, and seek to pull us down, we need a storage of faith that can carry youth and later adults over the dull, the difficult, the terrifying moments . . . and [the] years of adversity, want, confusion, and frustration."[13]

Finally, there are those who yield to doubt because they doubt themselves, doubt whether they have what it takes, doubt that they are *worthy* of eternal rewards, doubt whether they are celestial material. The Lord has not left us in the dark on these matters. We need not wrestle or wonder where we stand and whether our life is on course. We need not get caught up in weighing our good deeds against our sins or misdeeds. We could talk about how many things we need to do and how much improvement and transformation we must undergo to be prepared to dwell with God, but I believe it is really a much simpler issue.

President Brigham Young explained that if we are enjoying the gift of the Holy Ghost in our lives—that is, if we have what Paul called "the earnest [promise] of the Spirit" or "the earnest of our inheritance" (2 Corinthians 1:22; 5:5; Ephesians 1:14)—then we have God's sweet certification that we are on "saving ground," that we are living in what might be called a saved condition, and that if our lives were to be interrupted by death, we would enjoy an entrance into paradise and eventually into the highest heaven.[14]

The second major criterion is whether we hold or are worthy to hold a temple recommend. The temple is the earthly counterpart to paradise, and thus to be worthy to enter into the house of the Lord is to be worthy to enter into that place where our Lord dwells in the world to come. To be sure, if there are sins in our lives that need to be repented of, we dare not procrastinate that repentance (Alma 34:32–34). What the Lord asks of us is to live a spiritually balanced life, to point ourselves toward eternal life, to trust in the tender mercies and grace of Jesus Christ, to keep the covenants we have made in holy places, and to stay the course in the gospel path.

"If we die in the faith," Elder McConkie declared, "that is the same thing as saying that our calling and election has been made sure and that we will go on to eternal reward hereafter."[15]

Just before he was beheaded at the command of the emperor Nero, the apostle Paul wrote, "I have fought a good fight, I have finished my course, I have kept the faith: henceforth there is laid up for me a crown of righteousness, which the Lord, the righteous judge, shall give me at that day: and not to me only, but unto all them also that love his appearing" (2 Timothy 4:7–8).

Our Master, who finished his course and has prepared a place for us with him and his Father (John 14:2; Ether 12:33; D&C 19:19), yearns for us, as his followers and his disciples, to be finishers, to keep the faith to the end of our lives, and to join him in everlasting glory. God grant that it may be so with each one of us.

9

THE DECISION

In the early nineteenth century there grew up in the northeastern part of the United States a novel approach to preaching the gospel and making disciples. In a very real sense, it was a reaction to the high Calvinism of the day that emphasized God's total sovereignty and control over the infinite details of our lives.

Charles Grandison Finney, an attorney by training, built upon the concepts of the camp meetings so prevalent in that area, which became known as the "Burnt Over District" because of the fiery messages and baptisms by fire that had taken place. Finney came to be known as the master of revivalism, inasmuch as he treated the phenomenon of conversion as a science, a systematic program that could and did accomplish predesigned ends, namely, new followers of Christ. Indeed, Finney published pamphlets and books that explained in the minutest of details how to set up and carry out an effective revival. He became to revivals what Fanny Farmer became to cookbooks.

I mentioned earlier that Finney's approach to revivalism ran counter to the spirit of what John Calvin had taught: namely—that individuals were either saved or damned from the foundation of the world, that the atonement of Jesus Christ was efficacious only for the elect, and that those who were saved would be led and directed to accept the gospel. Those led to the gospel were not saved because they chose to be so but rather because God's sovereign will, the efficacious call, would always be realized, and that once they had come unto Christ they could never fall from that lofty state of grace. Finney's approach allowed more readily for individual moral agency and stressing that man and God were working together toward the salvation of the soul. The gathering place was prepared. The mood was established. The gospel was preached. The invitation on the part of the preacher was extended to the audience, and members of that congregation were fervently encouraged to "make a decision for Christ" or to "make a commitment for the Lord."

Thus, Finney is, in many ways, the real father of what blossomed and grew in the twentieth century as the revival or crusade for souls. It was altered and adapted over the decades but found its place in the late 1940s in the preaching and invitation of Billy Graham, perhaps the most beloved and traveled evangelist in the history of the world.

A typical Graham crusade would consist of the singing of traditional hymns, such as "Amazing Grace," "His Eye Is on the Sparrow," or "Just As I Am." Motivational messages from famous actors, athletes, or public figures who had "accepted Christ" would follow. Then the Reverend Graham would deliver a brief sermon (usually no more than twenty to thirty minutes) on such matters as the plight of our fallen world, our individual emptiness and need for forgiveness and spiritual wholeness, and the redemption that comes only in and through confessing our sins, accepting Jesus as Savior and Lord, and surrendering our lives to him. Dr. Graham would then invite members of large congregations (often packed stadiums) to come forward, gather at the foot of the podium, pray with him, receive Jesus in their hearts, acquire some literature, and then be encouraged to become more involved in a local church congregation.

Let's talk for a moment about how important the making of *a decision* can be. Decisions, when made in earnest and with one's whole heart, are extremely influential in our lives.

I decided to marry Shauna Sizemore in the Salt Lake Temple in 1971. I decided that I would love her, cherish her, pray for her, pray for us, provide for her, be a righteous example for her, and attend to her needs and deepest desires. Only she could say how well I have done that, but I have really tried to make her happy and secure. I did all of that because of a decision.

When I was very young I decided that I would observe the Word of Wisdom all my days and would abstain from alcohol, tobacco, coffee, tea, and habit-forming drugs. When I was at a military boot camp, we arose each morning at 5:25 to the jolting sound of reveille, dressed ourselves quickly, and made our way outside the barracks into formation. Then we would have a period of physical activity, including a one-to-two-mile run. I was in pretty fair physical condition, but I realized early on in camp that I had not done enough running in preparation for this daily ordeal.

More than once, when I was sorely tempted to drop out of our running formation and let the others go ahead of me, I found myself praying beneath my breath, "Father in Heaven, I need help, thy help. I cannot do this on my own. But I have lived the Word of Wisdom all my life and tried to keep my body in good shape. I now ask that the promise given—that we would run and not be weary—come to pass. Please give me strength." Well, I wish I could say that I then and thereafter became an avid jogger or a marathon runner, but frankly all that happened was that I made it through boot camp without failing the physical tests. I think of those weeks quite often, acknowledge completely God's hand in my tiny tender mercy, and realize once again that a decision, made a long time ago, resulted in a positive outcome.

My wife and I decided before we were married that our marriage would best be visualized as a triangle representing Shauna, Bob, and the Lord. Our individual lives and our marriage would belong to him. We decided that we would welcome children into our home, pay a full tithing, be active and involved in the Church, and accept and magnify callings. We have been married now for a little less than forty years and, despite the challenges and pain and vicissitudes of life that inevitably come to every marriage, ours has been a happy union. We have had our differences, our disagreements, our diverse views on things, but the idea of throwing in the towel and choosing to divorce has never been an option. We feel the influence of that Holy

Spirit of Promise, to whom it is given to bind and seal couples and families for eternity. We made an eternal decision. We have stuck with it. And that has made all the difference.

Almost thirty years ago a colleague and I were asked to read through, analyze, and look for patterns in a massive amount of anti-Mormon propaganda. It was drudgery. It was laborious. It was depressing. It carried a bitter and draining spirit, and consequently I had to just push my way through it to complete the assignment. After a period of addressing certain questions, my partner shook his head and indicated that the constant barrage of issue after issue was simply wearing him down and that he wasn't sure he could stick with it. I suggested that we were almost done and that a few more hours would be sufficient to make our report.

He stared at me for a moment and asked, "This isn't damaging to you, is it? I mean, you don't seem to be very upset by what we are reading." I assured my friend that obviously there were things I would rather be doing and that the hateful and contentious spirit did in fact weigh on me, but no, I wasn't particularly bothered by it.

"Why?" he asked.

"I can't say for sure," I responded. "It's ugly but doesn't really affect my faith."

Not long ago I had a conversation with a friend of another faith. She began to ask about my impressions of some anti-Mormon videos on the Book of Mormon and book of Abraham that had recently been released. I indicated that I had seen them and put them away.

"Bob," she asked, "this doesn't cause you to wonder if you're believing in a fairy tale?"

"Of course not," I replied.

"This doesn't make you doubt that Joseph Smith was a true prophet?" she inquired.

"Not in the slightest," I said.

"I just don't understand you!" she then added.

Later that night as I lay in bed, I rehearsed that conversation, which reminded me of the one I had thirty years earlier. I asked myself why I was not unnerved by attacks on the Prophet Joseph, the Church, or its teachings? Why don't these things challenge my mind or get to my heart? I wasn't sure.

I sat with my wife in our living room as we watched the April 2007 general conference. As I usually do, I took notes that would help remind my students and me of what was said—at least until the May issue of the *Ensign* came out. During the Sunday morning session, Elder Neil L. Andersen began his remarks by relating the touching story told by President Gordon B. Hinckley in the April 1973 general conference about the young

Asian man who had joined the Church while in the military and then faced the sobering realities of ostracism by his family and foreclosure of future promotion in the military.

"'Are you willing to pay so great a price for the gospel?'" President Hinckley asked the young man. Elder Andersen then related, "With his dark eyes moistened by tears, he answered with a question: 'It's true, isn't it?'

"President Hinckley responded, 'Yes, it's true.'

"To which the officer replied, 'Then what else matters?'"

Elder Andersen continued: "The cause in which we are laboring is true. We respect the beliefs of our friends and neighbors. We are all sons and daughters of God. We can learn much from other men and women of faith and goodness. . . .

"Yet we know that Jesus is the Christ. He is resurrected. In our day, through the Prophet Joseph Smith, the priesthood of God has been restored. We have the gift of the Holy Ghost. The Book of Mormon is what we claim it to be. The promises of the temple are certain. . . .

"It's true, isn't it? Then what else matters? . . .

"How do we find our way through the many things that matter? We simplify and purify our perspective.

Some things are evil and must be avoided; some things are nice; some things are important; and some things are absolutely essential." Then came the following words, which have changed my life and provided answers to the question: Why doesn't anti-Mormonism affect my faith?

"*Faith is not only a feeling; it is a decision,*" Elder Andersen said. "With prayer, study, obedience, and covenants, we build and fortify our faith. *Our conviction of the Savior and His latter-day work becomes the powerful lens through which we judge all else.* Then, as we find ourselves in the crucible of life, . . . we have the strength to take the right course."[1]

That was it. That was the answer. Faith is a *decision.* Decades ago I made a decision: I determined that God is my Heavenly Father. Jesus Christ is my Lord and Redeemer, my only hope for peace in this life and eternal reward in the life to come. Joseph Smith is the prophet of God through whose instrumentality the Book of Mormon, the Doctrine and Covenants, and the Pearl of Great Price—containing many plain and precious truths—have come. And he is the prophet through whom the keys, covenants, ordinances of the priesthood, and organization of the Church have been restored.

I decided that I would be loyal to the constituted authorities of the Church, that I would not take offense when there came either an inadvertent or intended "ecclesiastical elbow,"[2] as Elder Neal A. Maxwell called it. I decided that I was in this race for the long haul, that I would stick with the *Good Ship Zion,* and that I would die in the faith in good standing. No man or woman would ever chase me out of the Church. No unresolved issue or perplexing doctrinal or historical matter would shake my faith.

Now I suppose some would respond that I am either living in denial or am simply naïve to troublesome problems. I assure you that I am neither. I am a religious educator (and have been so for more than thirty years), am very much aware of seeming incongruities that pop up here and there, and I am a voracious reader. I spend a good portion of my time with people of different faiths, and some of them are ever so eager to bring to my attention questions intended to embarrass the Church or me.

But there are just too many things about The Church of Jesus Christ of Latter-day Saints that bring joy and peace to my heart, light and knowledge to my mind, and a cementing and sanctifying influence into my family and my interpersonal relationships for me to choose to throw it all away because I am uncertain or unsettled about this or that dilemma. To put it another way, the whole is much, much greater than the sum of the parts.

A tender scene in the New Testament comes to mind when I contemplate what it would mean to leave the Church or take my membership elsewhere. Jesus had just delivered the bread of life sermon—a deep and penetrating message on the vital importance of partaking fully of the person and powers of the Messiah. Many in the crowd at Capernaum did not understand and were even offended by the Master's remarks.

"From that time many of his disciples went back," John records, "and walked no more with him. Then said Jesus unto the twelve, Will ye also go away?" (John 6:66–67). What a poignant moment. Our Lord seemed to display a sense of disappointment, a somber sadness for those in the darkness who could not comprehend the light. Would he be left alone? Was the price too great to pay? Was the cost of discipleship so expensive that perhaps even those closest to him would leave the apostolic fellowship?

"Then Simon Peter answered him, *Lord, to whom shall we go? thou hast the words of eternal life.* And we believe and are sure that thou art that Christ, the Son of the living God" (John 6:68–69; emphasis added).

Once we have enjoyed sweet fellowship with the Christ, how do we turn away? Where do we go? What possible message, way of life, social interactions, or eternal promise can even compare with what Jesus offers?

Many years ago I attended a symposium where a number of presentations on the restored gospel were made, some of which were fairly critical of our faith and way of life. One man, a convert to the Church, spent the first two-thirds of his talk quipping about all of the silly, nonsensical, embarrassing, and even bizarre things that had happened to him since he became a Latter-day Saint. The crowd roared. The laughter over the Church and its programs was cruel, painful to hear, but nonstop for almost an hour.

Then the speaker became sober and said, in essence: "Now all of this is quite hilarious, isn't it? There are really some dumb things that happen within Mormonism. There are matters that for me just don't add up, unchristian behaviors that really sting, and situations that need repair. I think we all agree on that. But now let me get to the meat of the matter: I have spent many years of my life studying religions, investigating Christian and non-Christian faiths, immersing myself in their literature and participating in their worship. I have seen it all, from top to bottom and from back to front. And guess what—there's nothing out there that will deal with your questions, solve your dilemmas, or satisfy your soul. This [the restored gospel] is all there is. If there is a true church, this is it. And so you and I had better become comfortable with what we have."

He stepped down from the podium as silence reigned in the room. His message had struck a chord.

I was at an academic conference a few years ago when I was introduced to a woman who described herself as "simply Christian." She knew quite a bit about the Church but seemed intent on "ministering, evangelizing, and witnessing" to me. She stated that she admired the LDS people she knew and was particularly impressed with our emphasis on families. She then said, "But, Bob, clean living and strong families won't save you. Salvation is in Christ." I nodded my agreement but assured her that I was perfectly happy where I was. "But, Bob," she persisted, "there is so much that you're missing. There's so much we could offer you." At that point I decided to become more than a passive participant in the conversation.

"Okay, what do you have to offer me? What can you do for me? Why should I join your church or accept the tenets of your faith?" I asked.

"Well, first of all we could give you Christ," Betty said.

"That's wonderful, Betty, but I already have Christ," I answered. "I have surrendered my life to him and accepted him as Lord and Savior. I trust completely in the cleansing and transforming power of his atoning blood. I love the Bible, accept it as the word of God, and also accept the Book of Mormon as another testament of Jesus Christ."

"Well, then, we could help you be saved," Betty said.

"Betty, I have enjoyed a remission of my sins in the past, feel the sweet influence of the Holy Spirit right now, and fully anticipate being glorified with my family and living in the presence of the Father and the Son forevermore," I said. "My soul is at rest."

"I guess I just didn't know that much about Mormonism," Betty said. "Do you really believe all those things?"

"With all my heart. Now, would you like to know what my faith has to offer to you?"

Some years ago our Evangelical/LDS dialogue group—about twelve to fifteen of us who meet twice a year to discuss similarities and differences in doctrine—came together to consider the claim of Joseph Smith to be a prophet. The conversation, as always, was pleasant, cordial, and instructive. One of my Evangelical friends said at a certain point, "You have to understand that we as traditional Christians take the Savior's warning against false prophets very seriously. This is why we just don't jump on the bandwagon and accept Joseph Smith without serious reservations."

At that point I said: "We understand your position and can see where you're coming from. But that same Lord, in that same chapter, said something that is just as deserving of your attention and ought to be a significant part of your assessment of Joseph Smith. When it comes to judging prophets, 'ye shall know them by their fruits' (Matthew 7:16). The fruits of Joseph Smith, including the people, their manner of life, the lay ministry, the missionary effort, the temples, the charitable work of the Church throughout the world—these are things that cannot be taken lightly."

Some have wandered away because they did not exercise the faith that required a decision. Consequently, when something went wrong or something didn't seem to make sense, they chose to absent themselves from church meetings and eventually from the Church. President Gordon B. Hinckley extended an invitation and welcome to those who have left the fold:

"To you, my brethren and sisters, who have taken your spiritual inheritance and left, and now find an emptiness in your lives, the way is open for your return.

"Note the words of the parable of the Prodigal Son: 'And when he came to himself.'

"Have you not also reflected on your condition and circumstances, and longed to return?

"The boy in the parable wanted only to be a servant in his father's house, but his father, seeing him afar off, ran to meet him and kissed him, put a robe on his back, a ring on his hand, and shoes on his feet, and had a feast prepared for him.

"So it will be with you. If you will take the first timid step to return, you will find open arms to greet you and warm friends to make you welcome.

"I think I know why some of you left. You were offended by a thoughtless individual who injured you, and you mistook his actions as representative of the Church. Or you may have moved from an area where you were known to an area where you were largely alone, and there grew up with only little knowledge of the Church.

"Or you may have been drawn to other company or habits which you felt were incompatible with association in the Church. Or you may have felt yourself wiser in the wisdom of the world than those of your Church associates, and with some air of disdain, withdrawn yourself from their company.

"I am not here to dwell on the reasons. I hope you will not. Put the past behind you. . . .

"Try it. There is everything to gain and nothing to lose. Come back, my friends. There is more of peace to be found in the Church than you have known in a long while. There are many whose friendship you will come to enjoy. There is reading to be done, instruction to be received, discussions in which to participate that will stretch your minds and feed your spirits.

"The quiet longings of your heart will be fulfilled. The emptiness you have known for so long will be replaced with a fulness of joy."[3]

And so, if you have allowed unanswered questions in your life to develop into destructive doubts, I plead with you to think through the long-term implications of a decision to distance yourself from the Church. Ponder on what you are giving up. Think carefully upon what you will be missing. Reflect soberly on what you are allowing to slip from your grasp.

If you are one who is struggling with a doctrinal question or a historical incident, seek help. Seek it from the right sources, including your Heavenly Father. Be patient. Be wise. Assume the best rather than the worst. If you are an otherwise active member of the Church who finds himself overly troubled by something that should never have happened or something that can be remedied in your heart by simply recognizing that all of us are human and that forgiveness is powerful spiritual medicine, leave it alone. Let it go.[4] Keep the big picture and refuse to be bogged down by exceptions to the rule. Focus on fundamentals. Simplify your life and open yourself to that pure intelligence from the Spirit that is promised to us all—a state of mind and heart characterized by calmness and serenity.[5]

Alister McGrath has written: "Faith is basically the resolve to live our lives on the assumption that certain things are true and trustworthy, in the confident assurance that they are true and trustworthy, and that one day we will know with absolute certainty that they are true and trustworthy."[6]

Have you made a decision? Have you made *the* decision? Have you sought for and obtained a witness from God that the work in which we are engaged is heaven-sent and thus true? Such a quest is foundational to your future happiness and peace. Pursue it with fidelity and devotion. If you *have* received such a testimony, cherish it, cultivate it, and ask the Father in the name of the Son to broaden and deepen it. Then make the decision. Such a decision is a surrender to what you know in your heart of hearts to be true, even though you cannot necessarily see the end from the beginning. As you do so, you will enter the realm of divine experience and begin your journey down the path of faith.

10

⁓

BEYOND ALL DOUBT

Only a few months before I was to return home from a full-time mission to the eastern states, I stood one afternoon at the kitchen sink, washing and drying the dishes with my companion, a remarkably obedient and congenial elder who would be returning home in only a matter of days. We had enjoyed our time together very much, and the harmony and love that existed between us had a great deal to do with the success we had experienced in the area.

We were chatting about several things when suddenly our conversation turned to the celestial kingdom and what it would take to qualify for eternal life with God the Father and his Son Jesus Christ. At a certain point I shook my head and said, "Boy, I just don't know if I have what it takes. Do you?" This extremely humble and transparent but mature-minded young man looked me in the eye and responded, "Oh, come on, Elder Millet. I have every intention of inheriting the celestial kingdom. Don't you?"

At first I felt that his words might have been proud and haughty, but the more I thought about him and his life—he was raised on a farm, came from a large family, earned his money for his mission, was a deeply spiritual man—the more I realized that other forces were at work in his soul. After only a few moments of further discussion, it became clear that he wasn't boasting in his own accomplishments.

He was exulting in the fact that he trusted the promises of the Lord. He felt the influence of the Holy Ghost and knew that while he was not perfect, he was at least on course. He had made a decision many years earlier to follow the Lord Jesus Christ and to sustain and uphold his latter-day servants. His faith was as simple as that of a little child, but his confidence in who he was, whose he was, and what lay ahead was deep, profound, impressive, and life-changing for me. I longed with all my heart to feel that kind of confidence, and I set about to obtain it.

Elder Madsen was a bright young man, but he was no genius. He knew the assigned discussions and the scriptures well, but he was no budding theologian. He was able to stand at the door and bear a powerful testimony of the Savior and his gospel, but I do not suppose he could have provided an answer to every question that a local pastor or a visiting anti-Mormon could have put forward. In other words, he didn't have all the answers, but the answers he did have were sufficient to place him in good standing with God, sustain his faith in the Restoration, and motivate him to broaden and deepen his own understanding with the passing of years.

I have written at some length here about questions and answers, about doubt and peaceful assurance. It is inevitable that we will have questions throughout our lives—questions for which we will search and study and plead and converse. Many questions will be answered to our perfect satisfaction in this life, but other questions will be left unanswered until we pass through the veil of death and there gain the serenity and satisfaction that come through seeing life from a new and elevated perspective. We need not have doubts, or at least we need not have them very long. If I were to summarize and distil what I have come to know in the thirty-plus years I have spent in intensive gospel study, it would be this: *We must learn to feed our faith and doubt our doubts.*

We feed our faith when, like the sons of Mosiah, we become men and women of a sound understanding through searching the scriptures diligently, praying and fasting with earnestness and deep longing to know the things of God, and thereby opening ourselves to the mighty and merciful gifts of prophecy and revelation (Alma 17:1–3; see also Alma 5:44–47).

Sherem the anti-Christ "was learned, that he had a perfect knowledge of the language of the people; wherefore, he could use much flattery, and much power of speech, according to the power of the devil." Now note these words from Jacob: "And he had hope to shake me from the faith, *notwithstanding the many revelations and the many things which I had seen* concerning these things; for I truly had seen angels, and they had ministered unto me. And also, *I had heard the voice of the Lord speaking unto me in very word, from time to time; wherefore, I could not be shaken*" (Jacob 7:4–5; emphasis added).

Well, the apple does not fall far from the tree. Enos, the son of Jacob, knew very well the kind of man his father was. Enos knew of his goodness, his closeness to the Savior, and his profound knowledge of the Atonement and the principles of the gospel. He no doubt recognized—and I suppose I am reading between the lines—that his father had something he wanted, something most precious, something that brought strength and security and serenity into his life.

Therefore, Enos went into the woods ostensibly to hunt beasts, but in reality he went in solitude to hunt for the witness, the testimony, the sure knowledge that saves and satisfies the human soul. His prayers continued throughout the day and into the night—prayers in which he pleaded for a remission of sins, for that cleansing of the Spirit that brings peace and personal power.

Then came the voice of the Lord unto him: "Enos, *thy sins are forgiven thee,* and thou shalt be blessed." That gracious gift came to Enos, in the words of the Redeemer, "because of thy faith in Christ, whom thou hast never before heard nor seen. . . . wherefore, go to, *thy faith hath made thee whole.*" Having poured out his heart in sublime supplication, having received the desire of his heart, his "*faith began to be unshaken in the Lord*" (Enos 1:5, 8, 11; emphasis added).

Unshaken faith in the Lord. *Unshaken* faith in the work of the Lord. Isn't that what each one of us most desires in the midst of snide cynicism and religious skepticism? Knowing the truth and knowing that you know[1] bring peace and balance, certitude and calmness in a world gone mad. Indeed, to have a testimony of the gospel, to have put doubt out of one's life, is to have a settled conviction of things as they really are (D&C 93:24) and thus to enter the rest of the Lord.[2]

And so, be assured that if you and I are thinking and reflecting and musing, questions will arise. But we never need surrender to doubt. Indeed, "doubt focuses attention on ourselves and our anxieties and stops us from trusting in God. A preoccupation with doubt is just as pointless as a preoccupation with death: it doesn't change the situation, and it distracts our attention from the opportunities that the life of faith has to offer. . . . Preoccupation with doubt weakens or even cuts the lifeline between us and the living God. . . . Doubt is like an attention-seeking child: when you pay attention to it, it demands that you pay even more attention. This is a vicious circle that is difficult to escape from. If we feed our doubts, they'll grow."[3]

There remains but one thing more for me to do before I close—to bear personal testimony. I wish I were brighter, more intelligent, more incisive in my thinking and expressions. I wish I could read faster, comprehend more, absorb and remember larger amounts of material, and thereby possess the kind of broad perspective that would allow me to be a more effective teacher and a more competent disciple of the Lord Jesus Christ. In short, I wish I were smarter and that my native intellect were greater. But then I suppose it would be wise to take Alma's counsel and not sin in my wish; I ought to be satisfied with what the Lord has given me (Alma

29:1–3). And what he has given me is a witness, a conviction of the truthfulness of the restored gospel that is a strong, steadying influence in my life.

I know there is an all-powerful, all-knowing, and all-loving divine being because God has revealed himself—his love, his mind, and his will—to me. I know that our Father in Heaven has given us a great plan of happiness intended to cleanse and renew and remake every accountable man and woman on earth, to transform us from natural men and women to spiritual men and women, to conform us to the image of Christ and make us into new creatures.

I know that Jesus of Nazareth was and is the promised Messiah, the Redeemer of all humankind; that immortality and eternal life come in and through his atoning blood and in no other way; and that it is by the amazing grace of this Redeemer that we are empowered to "do good and become better" than we are.[4] I know Jesus lives because I know what it feels like to be washed in the blood of the Lamb, to be forgiven of my sins, and to be given a sweet foretaste of exaltation in the celestial kingdom.

A testimony of God and Christ must and should be brought up to date. Consequently, I say with all the fervor of my being that I know, by the same Spirit, that the Father and the Son appeared to the boy prophet in a grove of trees in upstate New York in the spring of 1820, that angels were sent from the courts of glory to bestow priesthoods and keys and powers, that visions revealing sacred doctrinal truths were opened to Joseph Smith, and that the keys of the kingdom of God, delivered to Joseph Smith during his twenty-four-year ministry, have been conferred upon his rightful successors in the presidency of The Church of Jesus Christ of Latter-day Saints.

I testify that the God we worship is the God who manifested himself to Adam, Enoch, Noah, Abraham, Moses, and Elijah. I affirm that the gospel we proclaim is not some other gospel or some false gospel but rather the glad tidings that salvation is in Christ and that peace and joy here and hereafter depend upon the manner in which we come to rely upon his merits and mercy and grace (2 Nephi 31:19; Moroni 6:4).

I bear my testimony to the fact that the Christ of the Book of Mormon and the Doctrine and Covenants is indeed the Christ of Matthew, Mark, Luke, and John. Our faith in the Lord Jesus Christ is neither ill-founded nor falsely placed. The central or fundamental message of the restored gospel is, as the Prophet Joseph Smith declared, "the testimony of the Apostles and Prophets, concerning Jesus Christ, that He died, was buried, and rose again the third day, and ascended into heaven; and all other things which pertain to our religion are only appendages to it."[5]

I do not yet have the answers to all my religious questions. Many items are still on the shelf. I fully expect to continue removing issues from the shelf and putting new ones up until the day I die. That is a vital part of my intellectual and spiritual growth. But while I do not have all the answers, I do have the conviction, born and bred into the marrow of my bones by the power of the Holy Ghost, that what I know, I know. It is neither myth nor metaphor. I have not given my life to a cause that is a hoax or a movement that is well-intentioned but misled.

Academics may smirk, skeptics may laugh, mockers may scorn, and attackers may seek to unsettle or embarrass the Church, but I rest secure in the divine promise: "Verily, thus saith the Lord unto you—there is no weapon that is formed against you shall prosper; and if any man lift his voice against you he shall be confounded in mine own due time. Wherefore, keep my commandments; they are true and faithful" (D&C 71:9–11). With me, it is the kingdom of God or nothing. I cast my lot with the prophets.

For many years I have prayed to receive answers to my questions. The Lord has been gracious to me and led me to people much more informed and to sources that have settled my discomfort. Because I spend a great deal of time on my feet delivering addresses and answering questions—from honest truth seekers as well as those bent on confounding me—I have not felt that I could enjoy the requisite spirit of gospel optimism and confidence if I were burdened or deadened by doubt. Consequently, I have pleaded earnestly with God through the years to banish doubt and fear from my mind and heart. He has heard my prayers. Further, he has answered my prayers. I know in ways more powerful than sight, in ways that transcend the five senses and the primitive pursuits of mortal man.

God grant that we may become a people mighty in faith, a people bubbling with enthusiasm to provide a reason for the hope within us (1 Peter 3:15), but also a people built soundly upon the foundation of faith and conversion. Indeed, the message we proclaim is Immanuel—God is with us—and with him at our head, the victory is assured.

NOTES

Preface

1. See Smith, Gospel Doctrine, 58, 126.

Chapter 1: Through a Glass Darkly

1. Smith, *Gospel Doctrine*, 12–13.
2. Lee, *Stand Ye in Holy Places*, 92.
3. Lewis, *Weight of Glory*, 106; emphasis added.

Chapter 2: Inevitable Questions

1. Scott, "Using the Supernal Gift of Prayer," 9.
2. Smith, *Teachings of the Prophet Joseph Smith*, 51.
3. McConkie, *New Witness for the Articles of Faith*, 5.

Chapter 3: Unnecessary Doubts

1. Smith, *Lectures on Faith*, 3:46; emphasis added.
2. Smith, *Lectures on Faith*, 4:13; emphasis added.
3. Smith, *Lectures on Faith*, 6:12; emphasis added.

4. Warner, "An Open Letter to Students," 16–18.

5. McGrath, *Knowing Christ*, 79.

6. Lee, *Stand Ye in Holy Places*, 77.

7. Maxwell, *Even As I Am*, 76.

8. Smith, *Gospel Doctrine*, 373.

9. Smith, *Gospel Doctrine*, 205–6.

10. McGrath, *Knowing Christ*, 79–81.

11. Cited in Lee, *Stand Ye in Holy Places*, 57.

12. Widtsoe, *Evidences and Reconciliations*, 31–32.

13. Packer, "What is Faith?" in *Faith*, 42.

14. Smith, *Lectures on Faith*, 1:15.

15. McGrath, *Doubting*, 133.

16. *Hymns*, no. 128.

Chapter 4: Seasons of Unrest

1. Woodruff, *Discourses of Wilford Woodruff*, 5; see also Smith, *Doctrines of Salvation*, 1:44.

2. Packer, "*That All May Be Edified*", 338; emphasis in original.

3. Lee, *Teachings of Harold B. Lee*, 139.

4. *Mother Teresa*, 1.

5. *Mother Teresa*, 1–2.

6. St. John of the Cross (1542–91) spoke of "the dark night of the soul" through which one passes as a part of the divine purification that brings about a union with the Lord. See St. John of the Cross, *Dark Night of the Soul*.

7. *Mother Teresa*, 33.

8. Steinmetz, "Growing in Grace," 10–11; emphasis added.

9. Pratt, in *Journal of Discourses*, 15:233.

10. Scott, "Using the Supernal Gift of Prayer," 9–10.

11. Hales, "Personal Revelation," 87.

Chapter 5: Leaning on Others

1. McConkie, *New Witness for the Articles of Faith*, 372; emphasis added.

2. Kimball, "Let Us Move Forward and Upward," 82.

3. Whitney, *Life of Heber C. Kimball,* 446, 449–50; emphasis in original.

4. McConkie, "'I Know That My Redeemer Lives,'" 36; emphasis added.

5. McConkie, "Purifying Power of Gethsemane," 11; emphasis added.

6. McConkie, *Promised Messiah,* 592–95.

Chapter 6: Using the Shelf

1. Smith, *Lectures on Faith,* 2:25.
2. Smith, *Teachings of the Prophet Joseph Smith,* 256.
3. Young, in *Journal of Discourses,* 6:281; emphasis added.
4. Young, in *Journal of Discourses,* 16:42–43.
5. Smith, *Gospel Doctrine,* 7; emphasis added.
6. Hales, "Personal Revelation," 89.
7. Maxwell, "'Answer Me,'" 32–33.
8. McConkie, *Doctrines of the Restoration,* 232.
9. Smith, *Teachings of the Prophet Joseph Smith,* 137.

Chapter 7: Doubting Our Doubts

1. Smith, *Gospel Doctrine,* 7.
2. Packer, "'Judge Not According to the Appearance,'" 79–80.

Chapter 8: Reservoirs of Faith

1. Smith, *Teachings of the Prophet Joseph Smith,* 278.
2. Smith, *Teachings of the Prophet Joseph Smith,* 268.
3. In Maxwell, "'Out of Obscurity,'" 10.
4. McConkie, *Mormon Doctrine,* 608.
5. McConkie, "Are the General Authorities Human?" 5.
6. Brigham Young, Heber C. Kimball, and Daniel H. Wells, in *Messages of the First Presidency,* 2:232.
7. Hinckley, "'Believe His Prophets,'" 53.
8. Hinckley, "Continuing Pursuit of Truth," 5.
9. Maxwell, *Plain and Precious Things,* 4.

10. Benson, *Witness and a Warning*, 13.
11. Benson, *Witness and a Warning*, 31.
12. Hinckley, *Faith, the Essence of True Religion*, 10–11.
13. Kimball, *Faith Precedes the Miracle*, 110–11.
14. Young, in *Journal of Discourses*, 8:124; compare 6:276; 1:131; see also McKay, *Gospel Ideals*, 6.
15. McConkie, address at funeral service for Elder S. Dilworth Young, 5.

Chapter 9: The Decision

1. Andersen, "It's True, Isn't It?" 74; emphasis added.
2. Maxwell, "Why Not Now?" 13.
3. Hinckley, "Everything to Gain," 95–97.
4. Packer, "Balm of Gilead," Nov. 1987, 17–18.
5. Smith, *Teachings*, 149–50.
6. McGrath, *Doubting*, 27.

Chapter 10: Beyond All Doubt

1. Callister, "Knowing That We Know," 100.
2. Smith, *Gospel Doctrine*, 58, 126.
3. McGrath, *Doubting*, 120–21.
4. Bednar, "Clean Hands and a Pure Heart," 82.
5. Smith, *Teachings of the Prophet Joseph Smith*, 121.

SOURCES

Andersen, Neil L. "It's True, Isn't It? Then What Else Matters?" *Ensign,* May 2007, 74.

Bednar, David A. "Clean Hands and a Pure Heart." *Ensign,* Nov. 2007, 80.

Benson, Ezra Taft. *A Witness and a Warning.* Salt Lake City: Deseret Book, 1988.

Callister, Douglas L. "Knowing That We Know." *Ensign,* Nov. 2007, 100.

Faith. Salt Lake City: Deseret Book, 1983.

Gibbons, Francis. *David O. McKay: Apostle to the World, Prophet of God.* Salt Lake City: Deseret Book, 1986.

Hales, Robert D. "Personal Revelation: The Teachings and Examples of the Prophets." *Ensign,* Nov. 2007, 86.

Hinckley, Gordon B. "'Believe His Prophets.'" *Ensign,* May 1992, 50.

———. "The Continuing Pursuit of Truth." *Ensign,* April 1986, 2.

———. "Everything to Gain—Nothing to Lose." *Ensign,* Nov. 1976, 95.

———. *Faith, the Essence of True Religion.* Salt Lake City: Deseret Book, 1989.

Hymns of The Church of Jesus Christ of Latter-day Saints. Salt Lake City: The Church of Jesus Christ of Latter-day Saints, 1985.

Journal of Discourses. 26 vols. London: Latter-day Saints' Book Depot, 1854–86.

Kimball, Spencer W. *Faith Precedes the Miracle.* Salt Lake City: Deseret Book, 1972.

———. "Let Us Move Forward and Upward." *Ensign,* May 1979, 82.

Lee, Harold B. *Stand Ye in Holy Places.* Salt Lake City: Deseret Book, 1974.

———. *Teachings of Harold B. Lee.* Edited by Clyde J. Williams. Salt Lake City: Bookcraft, 1996.

Lewis, C. S. *The Weight of Glory.* New York: Touchstone, 1996.

Maxwell, Neal A. "'Answer Me.'" *Ensign,* Nov. 1988, 31.

———. *Even As I Am.* Salt Lake City: Deseret Book, 1982.

———. "'Out of Obscurity.'" *Ensign,* Nov. 1984, 8.

———. *Plain and Precious Things.* Salt Lake City: Deseret Book, 1983.

———. "Why Not Now?" *Ensign,* Nov. 1974, 12.

McConkie, Bruce R. Address delivered at funeral service for Elder S. Dilworth Young. Salt Lake City, Utah. 13 July 1981. Typescript in possession of author.

———. "Are the General Authorities Human?" Address delivered at the University of Utah Institute of Religion, Salt Lake City, 28 October 1966.

———. *Doctrines of the Restoration.* Edited by Mark L. McConkie. Salt Lake City: Bookcraft, 1989.

———. "'I Know That My Redeemer Lives.'" *Ensign,* Jan. 1973, 36.

———. *Mormon Doctrine.* 2d ed. Salt Lake City: Bookcraft, 1966.

———. *New Witness for the Articles of Faith.* Salt Lake City: Deseret Book, 1985.

———. *The Promised Messiah.* Salt Lake City: Deseret Book, 1978.

———. "The Purifying Power of Gethsemane." *Ensign,* May 1985, 9.

McGrath, Alister. *Doubting: Growing Through the Uncertainties of Faith.* Downers Grove, Ill.: IVP Books, 2006.

———. *Knowing Christ.* New York: Doubleday Galilee, 2002.

McKay, David O. *Gospel Ideals.* Salt Lake City: Improvement Era, 1953.

Messages of the First Presidency of The Church of Jesus Christ of Latter-day Saints. Edited by James R. Clark. 6 vols. Salt Lake City: Bookcraft, 1965–75.

Mother Teresa: Come Be My Light, the Private Writings of the "Saint of Calcutta." Edited by Brian Kolodiejchuk. New York: Doubleday, 2007.

Packer, Boyd K. "Balm of Gilead." *Ensign,* Nov. 1987, 16.

———. "'Judge Not According to the Appearance.'" *Ensign,* May 1979, 79.

———. *"That All May Be Edified."* Salt Lake City: Bookcraft, 1982.

Scott, Richard G. "Using the Supernal Gift of Prayer." *Ensign,* May 2007, 8.

Smith, Joseph. *Lectures on Faith.* Salt Lake City: Deseret Book, 1985.

———. *Teachings of the Prophet Joseph Smith.* Selected by Joseph Fielding Smith. Salt Lake City: Deseret Book, 1976.

Smith, Joseph F. *Gospel Doctrine.* Salt Lake City: Deseret Book, 1971.

Smith, Joseph Fielding. *Doctrines of Salvation.* Compiled by Bruce R. McConkie. 3 vols. Salt Lake City: Bookcraft, 1954–56.

St. John of the Cross. *Dark Night of the Soul.* Translated by E. Allison Peers. New York: Doubleday Image Books, 1959.

Steinmetz, David C. "Growing in Grace." *Christian Century* 124 (30 Oct. 2007): 10.

SOURCES

Warner, C. Terry. "An Open Letter to Students: On Having Faith and Thinking for Yourself." *New Era,* Nov. 1971, 14.

Whitney, Orson F. *Life of Heber C. Kimball.* Salt Lake City: Bookcraft, 1973.

Widtsoe, John A. *Evidences and Reconciliations.* 3 vols. in 1. Arranged by G. Homer Durham. Salt Lake City: Bookcraft, 1960.

Woodruff, Wilford. *Discourses of Wilford Woodruff.* Edited by G. Homer Durham. Salt Lake City: Bookcraft, 1946.

INDEX

weakness, 11; are spiritually healthy, 13; no sin in having unresolved questions, 17; asking the right ones, 20; do not obsess over unanswered, 76; it is fair to question your questioning, 99; some remain unanswered in this life, 143

Revelation: Robert D. Hales on, 53; some things have not been revealed, 88; individual, from study of scriptures, 89; Joseph Smith on, 94; few people choose to leave the Church as the result of, 96; First Presidency (1865) on, 115

Revivalism: father of, Charles Grandison Finney, 123–25; description of Billy Graham's revival meetings, 126

Sacrifice, sign of obedience of Adam and Eve, 77

Salvation, striving for personal, 105

Scott, Richard G.: on receiving answers, 13; on prayer, 53

Sermon, the Bread of Life, 133

Sin: correlates with doubt, 33; member who desired

separation from Church is a story of, 34; blocks promptings of the Spirit, 43; some cannot let go of, 46

Smith, Joseph: on spiritual progression, 18; on Christian discipleship and sacrifice, 26; on doubt and faith, 26; on faith, 37; on the purposes of God, 77; on revelation, 94; on himself, 114; on the qualities of a prophet, 114; Evangelist-LDS dialogue group discuss, 136–37; Heavenly Father and Jesus Christ appeared to, 147–48; on the Atonement, 148–49

Smith, Joseph F.: on knowledge of premortality, 2; on spiritual laziness, 32–33; on humility, 33; on speaking in the Lord's name, 33; on receiving knowledge, 79; on being established in truth, 96

Snow, Lorenzo, on weaknesses in the leaders of the Church, 114

Spiritual progress: gauged by our willingness to see with eyes of faith, 30; a day-by-day process, 61

ABOUT THE AUTHOR

Robert L. Millet, professor of ancient scripture and former dean of Religious Education at Brigham Young University, has served as a bishop, stake president, and member of the Materials Evaluation Committee of The Church of Jesus Christ of Latter-day Saints.

He earned a master's degree from BYU in psychology and a Ph.D. from Florida State University in biblical studies and nineteenth- and twentieth-century religious thought. Before joining the faculty of BYU, he taught seminary and was an institute director in the Church Educational System. In addition, he has had experience in family counseling and social services work.

A popular speaker and writer, Brother Millet is the author of numerous books, including *Men of Valor,*

Grace Works, When a Child Wanders, and *Are We There Yet?*

He and his wife, Shauna Sizemore Millet, are the parents of six children.